THE GENIUS OF DIS

THE GENIUS OF DISCIPLESHIP

Dennis Gillett

THE CHRISTADELPHIAN
404 Shaftmoor Lane
Birmingham B28 8SZ
England

1984

First published 1984

ISBN 0 85189 109 8

ACKNOWLEDGEMENT

We thank Paul Wasson for the loan of
a colour transparency for the cover illustration: it shows young Christadelphians
walking in the English Lake District, and
demonstrating in action the disciple's
prayer (Hymn 88):

"Not for ever in green pastures
  Do we ask our way to be;
But the steep and rugged pathway
 . May we tread rejoicingly."

*Printed and bound in Great Britain
by Billing & Sons Limited, Worcester.*

PREFACE

A series of articles under this title appeared in *The Christadelphian* between January 1982 and February 1984 and evidently gave so much pleasure that it was decided to collect the parts together in book form. The author has, here and there, made a few changes; a new chapter, "Learning and Wisdom", which did not appear in the Magazine has also been added. Readers who followed the series will now have the satisfaction of seeing the work as a whole; all will now assuredly find delight and edification in these pages.

By a happy coincidence, the preparation of this book for the press came at a time when the Perth (Yokine) Ecclesia had asked the Christadelphian Office to suggest a new work which could be launched on the occasion of the Australian Youth Conference being held in Perth in January 1985. The organisers were happy to agree that this book, with its message for young as well as older disciples, would be a very suitable commemorative volume; accordingly we arranged for the first copies in Australia to be those destined for the Conference—sent with warmest wishes for its success.

In terms of relevance to the theme of the 1985 Conference, "Seek ye first the kingdom of God" (words displayed each month on the front cover of *The Christadelphian*), Brother Gillett's book has much to offer the disciple—especially the young disciple. There is in the chapter on "Perspective", for example, the following excellent advice on the ordering of his priorities:

"In the clear shining of two ways the genius of discipleship should lead us to be heavily biased on the side of the Truth, even though it may mean inconvenience, difficulty and even hardship. If this seems outrageous, the reader should understand that getting perspective right can be a painful process. It may mean looking critically at the importance we give to our careers, our families, our homes, our friends and our leisure . . ."

MICHAEL OWEN

FOREWORD

L ET there be no mistake. These chapters are not concerned to present the disciple as a genius. The genius is not in failing man but in the power of God. It is that process which transforms the disciple into the friend, the witness, the servant of the Master. It is that system of living which changes failure into fulfilment and finally into victory.

True discipleship involves the whole man and its influence should be conspicuous in every department of daily living. The objective is conformity of the disciple's mind and will to the image of Christ, so that finally, when the Lord comes again, the whole man, body, soul and spirit may be changed and fashioned like unto him, immortal and incorruptible. But now, while he tarries, the purpose is to create and develop faithful and consecrated souls, upon whom he can depend, through whom he may witness and by whom his cause is advanced in this world. The making of such through all the varied ways of life is the genius of discipleship.

G.D.G.

CONTENTS

1

"BE YE TRANSFORMED"

IS GENIUS the right word? Well, think what it means according to the dictionary. That says that genius is a creative faculty which is completely satisfactory—centrally the power of origination and completion. Used of discipleship, therefore, it means the central force of the calling, active for the purpose of transformation, because transformation is the objective of discipleship—now of the mind and character, later of the body. One of its foremost exponents once said, "Be not conformed . . . but be ye transformed by the renewing of your mind". This ought not to surprise us. The truth is that discipleship given full expression can change men's lives radically and redirect their energy and aspirations.

Saul of Tarsus is an excellent example: from being a hater and a persecutor he became a lover and an apostle. The strength he spent on cursing Christ was redirected and instead he crowned him King. To some of the Corinthian believers Paul wrote, "And such were some of you"; and what they had been is there in 1 Corinthians 6:11. He went on to say, "But ye are washed, but ye are sanctified, but ye are justified in the name of the Lord Jesus and through the Spirit of our God". This is the genius of discipleship—the central force of the calling, active for the purpose of transformation.

Probably most disciples would admit that the one thing which impedes transformation is the power of self. It shackles the spirit and brings good resolutions to dismal disappointment. The man from Tarsus understood it: "That which I hate, that I do." That is perhaps the saddest confession in the Bible. High purpose with no power; good intention mastered by impotence. Conscience may be

1

defective but it knows where the trouble is located. Sometimes men are maddened with anguish about their compulsive failure. Philosophy finds explanations in ancestry and environment.

These things are not without significance but the real trouble is deeper than circumstance, either of birth or every-day living. Somehow we know in our deepest heart that it is not in our stars but in ourselves that we are failures. Self, which ought to be the servant, is the master. No chicanery can change it. No fuller on earth can make this black into white. There is no quackery which can bring the all-sufficient remedy. Self-torture is no cure. Tinkering is not the answer. Rigour does not cleanse the heart. External adjustment is only an expedient. Short cuts are short on success. Some seek for victory by giving of their substance to good causes. Giving is a blessed grace and part of the genius of discipleship, but we cannot make up in generosity what we lack in spiritual strength.

In order to get to the central issue, mark the King's words: "If any man will come after me, let him deny himself, and take up his cross daily, and follow me" (Luke 9:23). This is fundamental—the record says he spake it to all. Of the three things enjoined, the last is a vital thing—to follow. The other two are utterly essential because through the essential you achieve that which is vital. The reason is this. You can approve, and not follow. You can applaud and not follow. You can understand and preach, without following. You can defend the Truth pugnaciously, without following. You can tire yourself out on busy works—without following.

Denial of Self

The central thing is the denial of self. It is utterly radical. Denial of self is the inward thing. Taking up the cross daily is the external manifestation of the inward condition. To talk of it is not to realise it. To write about it is not to achieve it. The use of the word *daily* emphasises that it is not just a theory but something that is real and practical; facing squarely every new circumstance; confronting bravely every impediment; grasping joyfully every new opportunity. In practice it means giving unhindered access to the Master into every chamber and especially into every dark corner. To think of that possibility might make us feel ashamed but at the same time it may do us good.

Consider that taking up the cross is not a fixed and static thing. It may mean different things for different people at different times. Sometimes the young man's cross is not the old man's cross. The principles abide—the practice changes. Cross bearing is not institutional, it is highly personal. It is *your* cross that has to be taken up, not your brother's. It is splendidly true that you may help your brother in his cross bearing, as Simon did Christ, but in the end each man's cross is his own. It is not Christ's either for he has borne his once for all, so that you may bear yours and not falter. Part of the genius of discipleship is recognising the cross in each particular life and facing it, not in misery, but gladly for love's sake.

The writer is increasingly impressed in discussions about discipleship that very often the battle has to be fought *over one thing*. As it was with the rich young man, "One thing thou lackest". The different things in different people may nevertheless be one thing in each case. The genius of discipleship forces the disciple to face the one thing. Without it there is no transformation. If Christ is to be accepted in the foreground every other thing has to be put into the background.

The Right Motivation

The list of priorities has to be radically re-arranged. If these words seem severe they are not as severe as the words Christ uttered: "So, therefore, whosoever he be of you that renounceth not all that he hath, he cannot be my disciple" (Luke 14:33, R.V.). The terms are so severe that they can succeed only if the motivation is right. Therefore reasons have to be sifted. Is it purely self interest? Is it to please some other person? Is it loyalty to some system? Is it to sustain a reputation? None of these is sufficient. It may sound trite but it is true—mastery is gained by crowning the Master as Lord and King. That means seeking to do all *for his sake*. That is the right motivation. That is why Paul came to write: "I am crucified with Christ, nevertheless I live."

Most disciples know about one particular temptation. It could be described as the desire to manipulate our understanding of discipleship so that we may keep the things which ought to be rejected; continue in the way of life which ought to be changed; retain the associations which ought to be severed.

3

True discipleship does not encourage impersonation. All the world may be a stage but disciples are not merely players. The terms are incisive and uncompromising—categorical and imperative. Said Paul: "Be ye transformed by the *renewing of your mind.*" Hence the use of the word genius—the dominant force which is creative in its effect. The process is not a repair job. It is not a course in window dressing. It is not making the best of a bad situation. It is not just a means of escape. It is not to enable us to endure what cannot be cured. Discipleship is a new thing, a new life based upon a new covenant. The vocation is at last to realise a new heavens and a new earth. Old things are passed away—all things are become new. Discipleship is concerned with a new man *created by God* in holiness and truth.

The New Man

"Follow me", said the King. The call is so simple, any child can understand it. Its meaning is so sublime that no philosopher, be he ever so clever, can exhaust the infinite meaning of the mystery—its genius. It is not misery—it is joy. It is not doubt—it is conviction. It is not fear—it is blessed assurance. Disciples are bond servants, but also friends who know their Master's will. They are not dragging themselves along reluctantly, hoping that their misery may win them some reward. They follow gladly for love's sake, trusting that because he lives, they will live also.

The genius of discipleship—the transformation—touches every aspect of life: being called, conviction, trust, surrender, purity, peace, prayer, service. In the chapters which follow, these things and others will be considered in the developing manifestation of the process.

2

ON BEING CALLED

THAT God calls people to the Truth there can be no doubt. The testimony is too clear to be disputed. Said Jesus, "No man can come to me except the Father which sent me draw him" (John 6:44). Paul wrote of "God, who hath called you unto his kingdom and glory" (1 Thess. 2:12). And Peter of Him "who hath called you out of darkness into his marvellous light" (1 Pet. 2:9). Said the Hebrew man, "Brethren, partakers of the heavenly calling" (Heb. 3:1). Said James, "Did not God choose the poor of this world, rich in faith?" (James 2:5). Said Jude, "To them that are called, beloved in God the Father and kept for Jesus Christ" (Jude 1, R.V.).

The call begins when the Gospel is heard and understood. It means that insofar as men repent it will be in response to the initial constraint laid upon them by God through His word. By the very nature of the case God takes the initiative. The invitation must precede the response. Faith is man's reaction to the revelation of Truth, but the truth comes from God. So God is the caller—man the responder. Understood in this way doubtless everyone would agree that God calls people to the Truth.

However, opinions vary and views diverge when it comes to what might be termed the *modus operandi* of God's call. Exactly what method does God use to confront men with the invitation? Roughly speaking there are two points of view about this. Firstly, there is what could be called the Individual Selection mode. This conceives of God as putting His finger on selected individuals and saying in effect, "I call you and you and you" and then arranging the circumstances in such a way as to confront them with the Gospel.

5

The other method could be called the General Preaching mode. This means that the Gospel is preached here and there, at home and abroad, under the control of God's witnesses, and all who hear it and understand it are being called. It seems to the writer that there is Biblical support for both points of view.

Take the case of Individual Selection. God called Noah to build the ark. He called Abraham to leave Chaldea and go to Canaan. Jesus called the twelve individually. The same could be said of Saul of Tarsus and some would be willing to add Cornelius, the Ethiopian eunuch, Lydia and the Philippian jailer. It has been argued that some of these were called individually and specially because they had special work to do.

In other words the call was not only a call to salvation, but also an election to service and that is why it was individual. With certain there is clear evidence that such was the case.

Chosen Vessels

Noah was called to build; Abraham to leave and travel. The Apostles are referred to as witnesses chosen before of God. Paul is called a chosen vessel to bear Christ's name before Gentiles and kings and the children of Israel. With regard to the others listed there is no Biblical evidence about an election to service but it may well be that they were special cases. Cornelius perhaps because he was a representative in that through him the door to the kingdom of heaven was opened to the Gentiles—the first Gentile to be baptized with the Holy Spirit. We could speculate that the Ethiopian eunuch was chosen to be the first preacher of the Gospel among his countrymen. Lydia perhaps had a special part to play in the service of the Truth—labouring with and offering comfort to those who preached the Word. We know nothing of the Philippian jailer after his conversion—but he is a remarkable man. In one hour he appears callous and brutal and in the next he is washing the stripes of his prisoners. What special purpose God had with him we cannot guess, but his conversion is very impressive. An earthquake and the Gospel in song and then the preaching of the Word.

Those who favour the General Preaching mode would point to Acts 2 and the great company of Jews, devout men from every nation, who heard the preaching of Peter and to whom the Apostle said, "Repent, and be baptized *every one of you* in the name of Jesus Christ" (Acts 2:38). That same day three thousand persons were converted. Soon after this, as the Word was preached, thousands more were added to the fellowship of the redeemed. Acts 8 records the great Samaritan campaign. It says Philip proclaimed unto them the Christ and the multitudes gave heed with one accord. There must have been a great many people involved for the chronicler to say, "Samaria had received the word of God" (v. 14). The Apostles decided it was remarkable enough to call for the sending of Peter and John. In Acts 14, in Iconium and other cities, multitudes were gathered together to hear the word of God and Paul speaks to them as though everyone was entitled to hear and believe and none was excluded.

God's Foreknowledge

In the parable of the sower the seed was broadcast in all directions and fell on varying kinds of soil with differing results. In the parable of the net it was cast into the sea and took of every kind. In the Apocalypse, we find these words: "*And whosoever will*, let him take the water of life freely" (Rev. 22:17). Jesus said, "If *any man* willeth to do God's will, he shall know of the doctrine, whether it be of God . . . " (John 7:17). Peter says, "God is not willing that *any* should perish, but that *all* should come to repentance" (2 Pet. 3:9). In Acts 10 Peter confesses with amazement, "In every nation he that feareth God, and worketh righteousness, is acceptable to him" (v. 35). This confession is preceded by the declaration that God is no respecter of persons. From these passages it looks as though all may come and none is barred if they accept the conditions.

Of course there are difficulties. Romans 8:29 is one: "For whom he did foreknow, he also did predestinate (R.V. "foreordained") to be conformed to the image of his Son, that he might be the firstborn among many brethren". In that passage the longest word, that is the word which goes furthest back is "foreknew". The word "predestinate" or "foreordained" refers to action taken as a result of foreknowledge. Notice that the action is the work God has undertaken so that those whom He foreknew may be able to conform to the image of His Son. Mark well that the foreordaining is to character. It is not an interference with the human will but to

7

enable the human will to be influenced so that the character may be in conformity to the image of God's Son.

This is to be effected in those whom He foreknew. Who are these? The whole teaching of the Bible tells us that they are those who believe, surrender and obey. The main objection is that the fact of God's foreknowledge must create necessity in the case of the human will. It is said that if God knows in advance then the freewill of man is obliterated. Not so. God is omnipotent: He can do as He pleases.

Man's Freewill

In creating man God limited Himself in respect of one thing but was limitless in respect of another. That is, He limited Himself in respect of the human will—He could, but He *would not* coerce men; He would leave them free to choose. However, at the same time He retained His power of foreknowledge—He did not limit Himself in knowing in what direction men would exercise their freewill. It means that because God is limitless He can limit Himself as and when He desires. He can foreknow without forcing men against their will. He foreordains that if they are to be His, they must conform to the image of His Son.

Romans 1:26 and 28 is another difficulty. God gave them up to vile affections; God gave them up to a reprobate mind. Those who know the Bible will know that this is a principle upon which God has acted always. There is a point in reprobation when God gives up the reprobates finally to their own choices. It was so with some Israelites in the Old Testament: "So I gave them up to their own hearts' lust: and they walked in their own counsels" (Psa. 81:12). We know that in this case for Israel as a nation the purpose was remedial. God gave them up so that He could gather them at last.

3

OUR CALLING AND ELECTION

IF God is willing that none should perish, why have so many never had the opportunity to hear the Gospel and respond? The majority are lost because of ignorance. As far as the writer is concerned there seems to be no answer to this problem. To say that men have no right to complain does not really answer the problem of the willingness of God on the one hand and the lack of opportunity on the other. We know for sure that God is taking out of the Gentiles a people for His name. Christ told his Apostles that they were to be his witnesses to the uttermost parts of the earth.

We must believe that whatsoever is God's will must come to pass eventually. Human neglect and human weakness cannot overthrow God's purpose. "So shall my word be that goeth forth out of my mouth: it shall not return unto me void, but it shall accomplish that which I please, and it shall prosper in the thing whereto I sent it" (Isa. 55:11).

Opportunity

It is a hard thing to have to contemplate that people are lost who could have been saved, because of human indifference. The whole teaching of the Bible is that those who are genuinely seeking the Truth in order to obey it, will find it. Said Jesus, "Ask and ye shall receive, seek and ye shall find, knock and it shall be opened". If this is not true then it seems we have been grossly deceived. Surely if someone seeks the Truth with a true heart, God will ensure that they have the opportunity to find it. Why the opportunity never comes to some we do not know. We cannot believe it is a matter of pure chance.

9

Again another problem. Would God call those who He knows will fail? We know it happened once. Judas was called as one of the twelve. This may be a special case, but the truth is that when the sower goes forth to sow—which is one method of the call going forth—the seed falls on inferior ground just as it falls on good ground. Put another way and to borrow a figure, when God points the divine magnet in this direction or that, according as His witnesses preach in this place or that, so sometimes the shallow mind responds as well as the deeper mind. At first the tares and the wheat respond together. This is another proof that God does not interfere with the human will in the matter of the final response. He calls, He woos, He invites—but in the end men are free to accept or reject the call.

So we come back to the two modes (individual divine selection on the one hand, and the work of general preaching on the other—see previous chapter) and in the end it seems that both have Scriptural support. What we have to be very careful about is the application of the Scriptural evidence in ways not warranted by the main teaching of the Bible. We can be sure of this: within the limits of human disability, man's will is free and he is able to choose. Once he is enlightened he becomes responsible. According to the Bible evidence God has called people to the Truth. Whether by selection or through general preaching it is a genuine call and in the end every call is individual.

Conversion

Thinking of today and the history of our community the emphasis does seem to be on individual experience. That is perhaps because most of the conversions have been in ones and twos. Sometimes the circumstances seem to be so deliberate. A man buys an old picture, removes the back and finds some *Bible Finger Posts*; he reads them and is converted. On a raw and gusty day a leaflet blows into the garden, is collected and the gardener is converted. In fairness we do not hear about those who buy old pictures and *Finger Posts* and who then ignore them; nor how many leaflets are picked up and thrown into dustbins with contempt. Notwithstanding, it does seem that some people are confronted with the Truth in strange and remarkable ways and in their deepest heart they believe that in those strange circumstances God was calling them to salvation.

Brother John Thomas is an example of this: called to salvation as well as elected to the task of unveiling the Truth in the latter days. On the other hand, very occasionally groups of people are called through general preaching. Once, years ago, in the writer's ecclesia, there were eighteen called at one time—all from a local chapel. Many young people are called through the teaching and influence of parents. The blessings of a godly home cannot be over emphasised. God uses the family as a means of confronting children with the Truth. Some people have said that because the Truth came so naturally through the circumstances of home training it does not seem to have the same impact as a tumultuous conversion in thrilling circumstances. In the light of the clear teaching of the New Testament to bring up children in the nurture of the Truth and to bring them to Christ, this estimate must be wrong. The call through the family is good and true and genuine. That is where Jesus began his life of faith.

Let us admit we cannot explain why some are not called and why some remain in ignorance. God knows—we do not. What we can and must do is to devote our attention to our own calling and election, and that of our brethren and sisters. It is the calling itself which is vital—the mode of it is secondary. There are variations in the details of the conversion: the one common fact is the radical difference Christ makes. In each is a new creation.

Men see according to what they are. Their outlook is a projection of themselves. Part of the genius of discipleship is a new conception of God and His purpose. The new conception results in a new attitude to living. They see their fellow men in a new light. They make their judgements by a new standard. They act from a new motive—for love's sake. They see God everywhere. The earth is full of the glory of the Lord. Fear ceases to be dread and becomes reverence. The grave becomes a quiet sleeping chamber. Homes become places of safety and delight. The ecclesia is a family— called to be a place of wisdom, godliness and joy.

"O the depth of the riches . . . "

What a wonderful thing the calling can prove to be! At the beginning it may be convulsive or placid. It matters not, because at the heart of it there is peace. There may be earthquakes but when the dust is settled there is tranquillity. All good is found in it. Thank

11

God you have received it. Many never do. Some come within touch of it who never lay hold. Sadly some will perish in spite of it. Let go everything, surrender everything, forsake everything that you may grasp it for ever.

4

CONVICTION

CONVICTION is a mysterious thing. There is no doubt about its source. "Belief cometh of hearing and hearing by the word of Christ" (Rom. 10:17, R.V.). The mystery is not in the source but in the working of the process. Here are two men, both intelligent, both men of integrity. Each reads the Bible regularly; each is known to the writer. Both accept the testimony of the Apostle Paul about the composition of man's nature in 1 Thessalonians 5:23: "I pray God your whole spirit and soul and body be preserved blameless unto the coming of our Lord Jesus Christ."

Two Attitudes of Mind

One is convinced that man is inherently immortal. He argues that if this is not true then man's part in God's purpose ceases to be rational. He insists there must be some form of conscious continuity between the life now and the life to come. He maintains that if this is not so—if death does mean total extinction as far as man's consciousness is concerned—then, he says, one personality strives and endures but another personality is rewarded with eternal life. He argues that it must be the same person in each situation, now and in the hereafter, and that person must be conscious of both conditions, else the reward has no meaning. Otherwise, he says, it becomes irrational and then uses a homely figure to press the point. It is like asking one dog to fetch the newspaper and then giving the bone to another.

The second man is convinced that man is inherently mortal and that such immortality as may come to him eventually will be utterly

13

conditional. He argues that death does mean total unconsciousness as far as man is concerned, but for those who are the subjects of resurrection there will be a genuine sense of continuity. That is, they will know who they are and will be able to remember and relate to their life before death, else how can they give an account of themselves to God at the judgement? Those who are rewarded are those who have endured and they will know it. There is continuity—in the mind of God continuously and in the mind of man when he is revived at resurrection.

Here is an interesting thing. Both men reach their conclusions from their own particular understanding of the Bible—sometimes from the same passage of Scripture. Take the case of the thief on the cross. The first man is convinced that when Jesus said to the thief, "Today shalt thou be with me in paradise" it was a clear promise that on that very day the dying thief would pass directly unto the bliss of heaven. He argues that to say otherwise is to be driven to dishonesty by the sheer clarity of the words themselves.

The second man says that to understand Christ's answer you have to notice carefully the thief's question. "Lord, remember me when thou comest in thy kingdom." The suppliant was looking forward to some day in the future when the Messiah would come again in his kingdom. Christ's answer, therefore, was saying in effect, "You are asking me to remember you in the day when I come again, but I give you my assurance *today*: when that time comes you will be with me in paradise—in my kingdom." The man says that Jesus used the word paradise because it represented all the things which were the very opposite of their then present plight. The garden of God—the place of peace, joy, tranquillity, life developing and life abundant. Christ was promising joy instead of pain, happiness instead of sorrow, life instead of death.

Distorting the Truth

To the Hebrew mind, and even to the thief, paradise meant this. The first man will have none of this. He says, politely, that it is an attempt to make the words of Christ mean something they were not intended to mean. Plain men are content with plain meanings. "Today shalt thou be with me in paradise" means today—this day, the day that began with this morning and ends with tonight. Today you will be with me in heaven, after we have both died and our souls have left our bodies. So each man thinks the other is wrong. Sincerely wrong, but wrong.

Our enquiry is concerned with why the first man does not share the conviction of the second. Man No. 1 honestly believes that man No. 2 has distorted the truth. Conviction is a mysterious thing. Sometimes it is conditioned a long way back. It is in this case. From the days of his youth and from the period of his university career he formed a strong opinion that man is a spiritual creature. That strong opinion developed into an abhorrence of the idea that man is an animal. Believe that and you have the first excuse to behave like a beast. So he clings tenaciously to the belief that man is a spiritual creature.

By spiritual creature he means that man is essentially spirit by composition. The body is a vessel, an earthen vessel fearfully and wonderfully made, in which the spirit, the real man, resides. He says to believe in his spiritual nature is to believe in his immortality. Those who deny his immortality must deny his spiritual essence. He also argues that man's universal desire for endless existence is presumptive evidence in favour of the fact. So the man comes to the Bible with this strong opinion and it is like a sieve through which every passage has to pass; a measurement by which every doctrine is graded. The nature of man, the destiny of the righteous, the fate of the wicked, the case of the ignorant pagan, the resurrection, the kingdom of God, the judgement, the coming of Christ, baptism, the nature of the Church—all are affected by the doctrine of man's inherent immortality.

Preconceived Ideas

In some cases the idea is fortified by a capricious selection of passages which can be pressed into giving support to the idea. It must be said that some people go through the Bible like a department store—choosing that which they like and leaving with the things which suit their taste. We believe that the doctrine of the immortality of the soul is a delusion, but not only a delusion: worst of all a snare, because it leads to so many other errors about the purpose of God.

So in this particular case the great hindrance to a right conviction of the truth is a preconceived idea, tenaciously held and which will not be shed notwithstanding the evidence against it. Rightly named, perhaps, this impediment is prejudice. After all, think what prejudice is: a judgement made by a distorted view of the evidence biased in favour of your own opinion; a humour of the soul which hides the truth. The thing to mark is that there is an element of truth in the preconceived idea. Man is not an animal. He is made in the image of God. Rightly understood, he *is* a spiritual creature. He is a rational personality, with the capacity to discern between good and evil. He is endowed with powers which place him at the summit of the creation. There is a great gulf between the highest animal and the lowest man. The fatal mistake is to believe that in this case spiritual means immortal.

Impediments to Faith

There are other forces which erect barriers against true conviction. Here is a short list: intellectual pride, idle speculation, worldliness, moral antipathy. Think about it. Intellectual pride is a condition of mind which cannot bring itself to admit that it might have been wrong; unteachable, because to yield to the teaching may mean giving up long held opinions and cherished ideas. Idle speculation regards the truth as an interesting theory—a subject for a pleasant discourse; a curiosity. The interest is shallow and superficial. Worldliness really means living as though this were the only world; a preoccupation with the material. The mind is dominated by things. Moral antipathy is a kind of self-induced antagonism which results in a frame of mind out of sympathy with the truth, because to surrender to the truth means an interference with habits and indulgences long established and firmly entrenched; a disturbance to carnal satisfaction which cannot be faced.

When you think of it, these are serious impediments. In experience they are not neatly separated as they are in analysis. People are affected partly by one and partly by another. In practice they are entwined. But they are always serious. The truth is not easily discerned by the jaundiced mind, mastered by pride and prejudice. Spiritual reality is not likely to be discovered by mere idle curiosity. The mind saturated by material influences is not often attracted to the things of the Spirit. Those who actually love darkness tend very much to hate the light. These are barriers to conviction. It does not mean that they are impenetrable, but penetration demands resolution, courage and humility. This sifts the contenders.

On the positive side, one thing becomes evident. In the process of coming to conviction a point is reached where the essential thing is a humble and receptive mind. The Bible insists that the truth is discovered most of all by lowly and contrite souls. To come in any other mood is to be greatly disadvantaged. It does not rest upon some accident of education or rank. Progress demands honesty, reverence and sympathy. Those who seek a new sensation, a material advantage, a cloak for self-advancement, are in the wrong department.

"The meek will he teach his way"

Conviction is a mysterious thing. It seems as though it can be communicated only to a certain kind of spirit. Jesus said a strange thing in John 18:37: "Every one who is of the truth heareth my voice"; as though there is a certain condition of mind and disposition of soul which is a prerequisite for conviction. The man who first heard the King's words was bitter, hopeless and proud. We may pity Pilate for his weakness, but Christ would not argue with him. There is a mood which muzzles sincere enquiry and there is a mood which liberates it. "The meek will he guide in judgment, and the meek will he teach his way" (Psalm 25:9). To seek the truth in order to obey it is the best mood of all.

Sometimes those who are confronted with the truth but will not yield to it find satisfaction in assaulting it. Sometimes the spirit which dare not say, "I have been wrong all my life", takes refuge in devaluing the agency which urged the enquiry. So the disputation turns to outright opposition. Angered by its logic they condemn the evidence and deny the word of God. Sometimes men are more anxious about being true to their principles than to ask whether their principles are true. It has happened that in order to be consistent they had to be false.

Always to be in doubt is an awful burden. Continual uncertainty is a weariness. A double minded man is like a ship without a rudder. Nevertheless, honest doubt is not a crime—and if it leads to conviction of the truth it is a blessing. So thank God that as part of the genius of discipleship we have found conviction. It is a great step in the long process of the life of faith; the root out of which other things can grow. We act according to what we are and what we are is regulated by what we believe.

17

Finally, let us anticipate a query. What about those who come to conviction and then eventually leave the truth? Does this invalidate the foregoing? Not so. The failure of the harvest does not prove that the germination was faulty. The parable of the sower testifies that there are other causes of failure. Conviction is not salvation. You can start right and end wrong. It is one thing to believe rightly but another to live in accordance with that belief. It is possible to confess high principles and then later on to live on low ones. That does not make the high principles nor the first confession of them to be false. Conviction is a vital step but it is not the whole story. This will be emphasised as we proceed.

5

TRUST

IT IS INTERESTING to notice how sometimes things which are true on the level of ordinary life are more intensely true in the life of the disciple. To illustrate: the idea that in order to wield authority you must first submit to it. If you want to exercise control you must first be controlled. This was realised at the ordinary level in the life of the Roman centurion. It was realised superlatively in the life of Jesus. This principle is especially true in the case of trust. Trust is the very foundation of ordinary life. Every day in every way we exercise trust. Life would be impossible without it.

When we start out in the morning we trust that the driver knows the way and will stop in the right places. When later on, with eagerness, we grasp the knife and fork we trust that what is set before us has been prepared without malice. We eat in trust. If we had to take time and seek means to test every dish for poison we should starve. The whole world of business holds together in a great system of mutual trust. Men trade and give credit on trust. The acquisition of knowledge is based on trust. We trust our teachers. We accept from them truths which we have no opportunity to prove.

It is strange that sometimes the things we are most sure about began simply by an act of trust. There is no progress in anything without trust. The most intimate relationship in ordinary life begins with trusting the first whispered assurance of love. Homes are homely because of trust. Jealousy and suspicion make them places of torment. Trust brings joy and confidence. Friendship is based upon trust. If your brother cannot trust you how can you be his friend? The worst place in the world must be the place where there is no trust—a place mastered by despair. So all aspects of ordinary life seem to testify that the universal demand is for trust.

All this is intensely true in the life of discipleship. It is trust which turns conviction into faith. It is one thing to declare that a rope is strong; it is another thing to rest your weight upon it. Conviction is essential but it is not the whole story. It is one thing to believe the truth; it is another thing to act upon it. Trust is faith in action. Faith sometimes is a theological expression, but in its development it becomes highly personal. Faith is the conviction that God is a rewarder of them that diligently seek Him. The declaration without the diligence is on the way to being only half true, perhaps even half false on the lips of the one who confesses but will not trust.

"Evidence of things not seen"

Ponder the verbs of Hebrews 11. Abel offered; Enoch walked; Noah was moved with godly fear; Abraham went out; Moses endured. The writer has heard it explained as all a matter of simple faith. Rightly understood that is true, but the inference is that because the faith is simple, it is therefore easy. Whoever says it is easy has misunderstood it. It was not easy for Noah to build a big liner in the middle of dry land. It was not easy for Abraham to leave a settled life and face the wilderness in search of a land he had never seen and which he did not know. It was not easy for Moses to surrender a prince's life to take his place with those in bondage. It is not for nothing that Paul urges us to fight the good fight of *faith*.

Disciples may be glad to fight, but it is not easy. It takes grit and force and trust. Trying and trusting are complementary. Trust is the optimism of faith. To all human seeming the optimism is unwarranted, but to the man of faith it is a perfect certainty. Trust is what the writer to the Hebrews meant by the evidence of things not seen. Trust has the effect of proving the invisible. It makes us put confidence in the declaration and venture trustingly upon the suggestiveness of the promise. The result is an assurance of things hoped for. Trust is a risk, a venture, an adventure. It has in it an element of inspiration. It is not blind, blundering chance. Faith, after all, is not ignorant assumption—the right name for that is superstition. Faith is intelligent trust.

Why was Abraham so sure of the unknown land? Because he was utterly sure of the unseen God. John in Patmos had a vision of a city. It is more beautiful and more wonderful than any other. As we believe in it and trust it we know in our deepest heart that we are brought into fellowship with the future. Trust in the things not seen gives us assurance of things hoped for. Our trust is not in pundits, parliaments or policies, else we should be of all men most pitiable. Nor should our trust be circumstantial, at the mercy of every passing change. It should venture as strongly in December as it does in June. Trust in the things which cannot be shaken should bring constancy in the midst of the changing scenes of life. Through the contradictions, the adversity, the apparent denials, God bids us trust. We do not always know the reason for our disturbance but we know the disturber. We can trust Him.

The Touch of Faith

Think of Luke 8 and the woman with an issue of blood. In the midst of the jostling crowd the King said, "Who touched me?" The question is a revelation. A hundred people had touched him but one had reached him in a way the others had not. It was the touch of faith. Notice this—it was a touch which under the compulsion of love he was obliged to answer, notwithstanding the urgent business before him on behalf of Jairus. By the touch of faith one soul was separated from the multitude and came to personal recognition by the King. Think of the one who was separated. Twelve years of suffering; twelve years of ostracism; twelve years being cut off from fellowship. She had heard that this man healed the sick and strengthened the weak. She was weak herself but she struggled to the front row, breathless and excited. The man from Nazareth passed by and she touched him. We can speculate that it was more than a fingertip touch. The urgency of the need would strengthen her hand. People in agony are people ready to grasp for help. So she clutched the border of his garment. The thing to understand is that she ventured upon the testimony which she had received about this man. That is she touched him hopefully—tremblingly, but trustingly. No doubt part of her hope was that she would be undiscovered, a woman who came and hoped to creep away.

But faith is not generated in order to be hidden. Secret testimony is not the best testimony. The disciple is expected to confess his

Lord in the open. The Lord had already said a few days before that nothing is secret that shall not be known. Those who believe should come into the light. It is one thing to see the King as he passed by: it is a better thing to meet him face to face. Her trust was justified. It must have been a complete cure. This physician does not dispense his healing in little boxes. She would not need a second opinion. He said, "Thy faith hath made thee whole; go in peace". Whatever he did, he did splendidly. But there was another blessing. He called her "Daughter". To an ostracised woman that word is music. To one out of fellowship it has the ring of tenderness. The lesson is this—for those who venture in trust there is a blessing. If you act in faith you may discover the secret things of his fellowship.

It has been pointed out more than once that the miracle on the woman must have had a profound effect on Jairus. The woman had been ill for twelve years, just as long as his daughter had lived—and now she was dead. Twelve years and then a miracle. Jesus said, "Fear not! only believe". It is another way of saying, Trust me. Perhaps Jairus went to his home with a lighter step—a weight already lifted from his heart, ready to believe. It shows us that faith is not just for ourselves. The faith of one disciple can help another. That is why Hebrews 11 is so good for us. Perhaps your confession of trust can help some Jairus, facing adversity, anxious and smitten. Sometimes trust is infectious.

We Trust because we Know

The Psalmist says: "They that know thy name will put their trust in thee" (Psa. 9:10). The reason for trust is in what we know of God. The warrant of faith is the Divine character. Because God is righteous He cannot do wrong. Because He is love He can only act lovingly. Unbelief will try to deny this—but have none of it. In spite of the anguish and the trial, we believe that God is trustworthy. He loves to be trusted. In the final analysis that is what He asks. Not that we explain Him, defend Him or vindicate Him—but that we trust Him.

For God and man trust is the most precious thing to possess: the quality that makes life possible in every sphere of existence, high and low. Trust is a mighty thing. It is a vital part of the genius of discipleship.

6

SURRENDER

IN this case there is no need for any esoteric definition. Here the word means what is usually means. Surrender is handing over control to another; the relinquishing of power to some other authority.

Think of it in this way. The life of discipleship is like a citadel. The disciple is the keeper; the King is seeking control. The aim of the King is sovereignty over the whole building. He desires access to every room and every passage, from the basement to the tower. He urges surrender but he will not compel. He entreats but will not drive. He will use every circumstance to encourage and make every obstacle a stepping stone—if the keeper will cooperate. The keeper has made a commitment to cooperate. In principle he has made the surrender; in practice he is reluctant to submit. Some rooms are locked against the King. Some doors are marked private. Some entrances say, "Keep Out". The keeper says he must retain some independence. There are some things about which he must please himself; some areas where his preferences must prevail. The King is not a burglar. He knocks but will not trespass. He calls but will not coerce. The King is patient. Sometimes he has waited a human lifetime for doors to be opened. He knows the keeper well. The keeper has disabilities at both ends of his constitution. He has a bad memory and he has foot trouble. His mind wanders and his feet have a way of going in the wrong direction. The King says there is a remedy for human disability, if the sufferer will surrender to the treatment.

The King and the keeper have a regular appointment to discuss advancing the surrender. The King is always there—the keeper too often is absent. He is so busy with things outside the citadel. Sometimes he is locked in the private apartments, by his own will and for his own purposes. He insists on retaining the master key. Sometimes he is irritated by the King's knocking, embarrassed when he thinks of the King's presence, glad that the latch is on his own side of the door. The keeper says that not all keeping is bad—there are some things he must keep for himself. The King says that the laws of his service are different; measured by the keeper's standards even paradoxical. Those who surrender are set free. Those who keep their life, lose it. Those who lose it for the King's sake, find it.

The keeper regards this as a fascinating theory. Sometimes he will discuss it at length. The philosophy makes him feel good. The reality makes him feel afraid. He is sustained in his reluctance by the suspicion that the King will want to make changes. The keeper does not like disturbance and the King is a disturber; he does not ask if it is convenient. The keeper says he intended the citadel to be a place of comfort and security. The King says he is more concerned about health than comfort. He says the keeper ought to be ready to be disturbed, because that is the way to be truly undisturbed. Loins ought to be girt and lamps ought to be burning. With this the keeper agrees but he is nervous about the exposure; he feels safer in his own room with his own things and looking after his own affairs. There are times when he feels bad about ignoring a claim which in his heart he approves.

Surrender is no Walk-over

The King and the keeper both know that surrender is no easy thing. So the King persists. Notwithstanding the setbacks he holds the keeper close to the ideal. Gently he removes obstacles or places obstacles in the way—all to advance the cause. As the days go by the keeper will flinch less and trust more. Latches will be lifted and doors will be opened. One day the King's sovereignty will be unchallenged and the citadel will be under new management.

Let us leave the parable and come to a real live case—the young ruler in Mark 10. He is not a disciple when we meet him but his case is significant because it has to do with the unsurrendered thing. He was a man with a clean record and anxious to find a life more satis-

fying than living as a rich young ruler—a man of genuine aspiration
and fine temperament. To him Christ said: "One thing thou
lackest." That was the thing he needed to surrender because it was
the one thing which stood in the way of discipleship. It is a superficial interpretation to say he lacked poverty. Just to be poor is not
the passport to eternal life. Christ could see that in spite of his
aspirations this man was mastered by his wealth. No man can serve
two masters. If you have surrendered to one force you cannot be
mastered by another.

What he really lacked was the right master. The dominating principle of his life was gold and it should have been Christ. He had
bent his will to the wrong throne. He needed to reject the thing that
mastered him so that he could become the bondservant of the King.
"Sell all that thou hast and give to the poor, *and come and follow
me.*" Without the first he could never do the second. His citadel
was unsurrendered whilst he was buried under a heap of gold. To
say "Follow me" is to ask for allegiance. To give allegiance is to
surrender.

A Drastic Remedy

It was not just being rich that constituted the impediment. After
all wealth is a relative thing. A poor man here would be a rich man
somewhere else. His wealth was the means of providing all the
things which ministered to his indulgence. As far as we can see he
could not surrender this advantage. It is not just having money
which is so attractive but the chances which the money brings: the
opportunity to enjoy all the things which the flesh and spirit desire.
This he could not relinquish. Christ's remedy was drastic because
the need was drastic. There are some things which you cannot
tinker with. To sell and give half his goods to the poor would have
left him just half as rich as before, but still wealthy—enough left to
satisfy all his selfish desire.

In this case the remedy had to be daring and radical. It called for
heroism and courage. Notice the sweet paradox in the voice of the
King—"and thou shalt have treasure in heaven". The surrender
would effect a transfer of treasure from the earthly bank to a place
where rust cannot corrupt and where thieves cannot steal. Let it go
in order to increase it. Lose it and you will find it. We do not know
for sure what he did at last. But we can be sure of one thing— he

was never the same again. No man ever is who comes as close to life as this.

The word of Christ to us may not touch our bank balance at all. But he will put his finger upon the one thing which, if we do not abandon, we shall never be able to surrender in the final sense. It is the thing which it is difficult for us to master and which is in danger of mastering us. So he is saying: "Go and . . . " The writer does not know what follows but you can be sure he must know for himself. If men or women give themselves five minutes of honesty they will know. They may not like the revelation but they will be that much better for the knowing. It is the thing which stands between us and the full realisation of "Follow me". Seek the testimony of those who have been confronted and have surrendered. They will tell you that in the doing of it they found their life. Unsurrendered life is life in the basement and in the darkness. Surrendered, it is life in the tower and in the light.

The Examination

In practice it may have to be drastic if you mean business. The King has prepared us for this. "If thy right hand offends thee, cut it off. If thy right eye offends thee, pluck it out." Could it involve father, mother, wife, child? some good thing which has become a curse? some indulgence which is sapping your strength? some association which is leading you away from the Truth? some ambition which is ruining your character? some flirting with temptation which is enticing you towards perdition? some shutting out of the light which is stifling your conscience? Or again, it may not be anything like this. Perhaps some simple neglect of the things which ought to have your whole attention; some weariness which interferes with faithful service; some doubt which cramps your energy and your devotion.

Whatever the impediment, the King urges us to surrender ourselves to him without reservation. In that surrender we can find salvation and sanctuary.

7

PARDON

WHEN all is said and done, disciples are individuals and they differ from each other in many ways, but in one thing they are all alike—they all need pardon. Whether it is the first pardon through baptism or the continuing pardon through the daily life of discipleship, the principles are the same. This chapter is concerned especially with the pardon needed and sought at the end of each day or each week. The forgiveness of the natal day is crucial, but just now we are concerned with the need for pardon in the developing experience of discipleship.

With some people it is fashionable to say that pardon is full and free and unconditional. It is full and free but there are conditions. It is not a rubber stamp. Pardon is for those who repent. The conditions are not arbitrary—they are an essential part of the process. It is difficult to save a drowning man if he will not surrender to the life-saving rules. The analogy is not perfect, but what is difficult with the drowning man is impossible with the sinning man if he will not surrender to the life-giving principles. Men cannot be pardoned against their will. So, rightly understood, pardon is conditional.

Think of the conditions. Firstly, there must be confession. John says it plainly: "If we confess our sins he is faithful and just to forgive us our sins, and to cleanse us from all unrighteousness" (1 John 1:9). Next there must be contrition. The psalmist says it in a psalm which is all about forgiveness: "A broken and contrite heart, O God, thou wilt not despise" (Psalm 51:17). Paul said it to the Corinthians: "Godly sorrow worketh repentance to salvation" (2 Cor. 7:10). Sanctified common sense teaches us that there cannot

27

be repentance if there is no regret. Then thirdly, there must be a purpose of amendment—that is a striving to avoid committing again the sin for which pardon is sought. Pardon is not conditional upon never committing the sin again; it is conditional upon the intention not to do so being genuine.

The writer remembers an old story about a last minute reprieve for a condemned man. Before it was handed over, the condemned man was asked what he would do if he were set free. He said that he would kill the judge and the chief witness. The reprieve was cancelled, because pardon is for the man who is prepared to quit sinning, given the chance. To seek cleansing with the intention of getting back to the old sin is to invalidate the process right at the start. Peter says it and uses a shocking figure to press home his words. He says it is like a dog returning to its own vomit. So there must be a sincere intention to reform. Pardon is not licence to go on just the same as before. In practice it has to be admitted that we are compelled to confess the same sins time and again.

Notwithstanding, it is one thing to strive for success and fail through weakness, sorrowfully hating the failure. It is quite another thing to fail through seeking the occasions of sin deliberately. It is one thing to blunder through ignorance or inexperience; it is quite another to blunder through flirting with temptation unheedingly. Nobody can be blasé about sin. So there must be a firm purpose of amendment.

A Forgiving Spirit

Then fourthly, pardon demands a forgiving spirit towards others. Jesus said it categorically: "For if ye forgive men their trespasses, your heavenly Father will also forgive you" (Matt. 6:14). He goes into detail about the forgiven servant who was himself unforgiving and the judgement that came upon his hardened heart, saying, "So shall my heavenly Father do unto you, if ye from your hearts forgive not every one his brother" (Matt. 18:35). This teaching is reinforced by the case in Matthew 5 of the man offering a gift at the altar and then remembering he is estranged from his brother. He must leave the gift and grant his brother pardon before the offering can be received in heaven. So finally, if you seek pardon you must grant it to your brother first. Whilst it is withheld forgiveness of your sins is hindered. Pardon is conditional.

Come back to confession. Psalm 32 is revealing about this: "Blessed is he whose transgression is forgiven, whose sin is covered. Blessed is the man unto whom the Lord imputeth not iniquity, and in whose spirit there is no guile." What is guile in this context? It is the attempt to hide or cloak over the offence. It is keeping silence when we ought to be open and frank. It is deceit in order to conceal. At first sight it might be said that it is impossible to use guile with God—but we do. How often are we saying that the bad things we do are not as bad as they seem! How often are we giving fine names to doubtful practices in order to make them plausible? How often are we saying, even in our confession, that we did this thing, but so would plenty of other people in the same circumstances? In one way or another, how often do we try to justify the faults in order to make the confession easier and the guilt lighter?

No Hiding-place for Sin

This is guile and it is guile with God. From Psalm 32 it is evident that where there is guile there is no pardon. Reading it very carefully, the impression is gained that the guilt is fixed even firmer when guile is practised. It is one thing to sin. It is a worse thing to justify it or by stealth to seek to hide it or deny it. The Psalmist says that when he did this something strange happened to him: "When I kept silence, my bones waxed old through my roaring all the day long. For day and night thy hand was heavy upon me: my moisture is turned into the drought of summer" (vv. 3-4).

It looks as though when he was trying to hide the sin, to forget it and submerge it, God gave him no rest. The hand of God troubled him. He wanted to silence the memory of the deed, but the consciousness of it was kept alive in his mind by God and there was no peace. God made the dark sin to haunt the sinner. God would not let him escape to oblivion. When he was ready to forget, God sustained the controversy. To put it bluntly, the sinner was miserable. Notice the figure he uses to describe it: "My moisture is turned into the drought of summer." The picture is of a tree without sap, withered and wasted; a living thing, drought-stricken. This was God's method with a man who would not acknowledge his sin. It may seem severe—it is severe but full of caring compassion. Mark the outcome: "I said, I will confess my transgressions unto the

29

Lord; and thou forgavest the iniquity of my sin" (v. 5). The thing to notice is how quickly God responded. As soon as the man resolved upon confession the pardon came. "I said . . . and thou forgavest." It did not have to wait until the penitent was in the secret place on his knees. It was not delayed until the Sabbath service. As soon as the guile was abandoned the sin was forgiven. When deceit was ended, the pollution was cleansed. At the very moment the attitude of submission is revealed, God acts.

This accords exactly with the parable of the prodigal son. When the boy said, "I will arise and go to my father", the father went out towards him. There was no waiting until he came and knelt and did penance. Even his confession was smothered with love. Pardon is a swift grace when the obstacles are removed. In a moment, at the twinkling of an eye, as fast as light and faster, as gentle as the first flush of dawn, upon the guilty man is pronounced the verdict of freedom.

The Mercy Seat

Guile is one impediment to pardon. Think of another—an unforgiving spirit. The man in Matthew 5 is drawing near to the altar. It must be recognised that the prime purpose of drawing near is to find pardon. The altar is the place of the mercy seat. The King tells us a remarkable thing; that at the altar there is no place to hide. It is a place of refuge but not a place of deception. There men are in the light. There is no provision for cloaking the truth. It is the place for confession but not for excuses. Jesus says it is the place where the will is provoked to action. Examination of the heart in the presence of the mercy seat brings to light an impediment: an unhealed rift in the life of the penitent. The gift must wait. It would be no good to hasten the offering.

To go forward is to move backward. Jesus says: "Leave there thy gift before the altar." Here is the mystery. To go to your brother is to draw nearer to God. As a result of going you may have to crucify your pride but that is what it deserves. Remember it is not just for your own sake you go, but also for your brother's. Your forgiving spirit will ease his resentment. His pardon will end your fever. As you confront each other in the spirit of loving forbearance, a great blessing is being prepared. Listen to the welcome: "then come and offer thy gift". The grace of God can now flow. The repenting man is now open, honest, sincere. He is in the light and therefore there is fellowship with heaven. Absolution is granted because he has forgiven his brother.

Vital for Pardon

Remember how vital this matter is. An unforgiving spirit means there is no pardon for your other sins. A rift fostered when it could be healed is a curse upon the life of faith. Neglect hardens the conscience. The mind becomes morbid and multiplies the ill-will. Grace is deferred and guile expands. The need for pardon is calling every disciple to examine at the altar his feelings towards God's other children. An unforgiving spirit means that the desolation of unforgiven sin abides and grows. Here there is no room for negligence. It is too serious and the resulting failure too solemn. We cannot win pardon; we can only receive it gladly and gratefully. Let every troubled heart remove the impediments to pardon and receive it joyfully and find peace.

8

PURITY

JUST as all disciples are against sin, so all disciples are in favour of purity. But all disciples know it is easier to denounce sin than to renounce it. Most would confess that it is easier to approve purity in principle than to perfect it in practice. To be convicted of impurity seems worse than being convicted, say, of covetousness. It is not worse necessarily but it seems worse. It appears more shocking. Why is this? Because in the minds of many people impurity has a strong sexual connotation. This is understandable, because sexual permissiveness does lead to a great deal of impurity.

But there is other carnal conduct apart from sexuality. There is greed and gluttony and sloth. There is the cry of the mouth, there is the seeking of the eye, there is the grasping hand. There is the allurement of temptation. There is envy, jealousy and lust. By these things discipleship is tainted. Purity, therefore, is a condition free from contamination and pollution. Positively it is clean, chaste, unsoiled. The absolute tone of those adjectives drives home the realisation that it is easier said than done. As an example, think of this. We sometimes speak of having pure motives. Who dares to say that his motives are always pure? No secret selfishness; no hidden self-esteem; no veiled pride? So although we may be satisfied that we are free from sexual impurity, wisdom should warn us that there are other kinds which have to be recognised and repudiated.

Purity demands Resolution

There are three passages of Scripture which bear powerfully upon this subject and which ought to be pondered carefully. The first is in 2 Corinthians 7:1: "Having therefore these promises, dearly beloved, let us cleanse ourselves from all filthiness of the flesh and spirit, perfecting holiness in the fear of God." The first thing to notice is that the motive force in the process of cleansing is not human strength but divine influence. "Having therefore these promises." The power is in the promises and the claim that faith makes upon them. To strive for the cleansing and to neglect the promises is to court failure. To accept the promises and to neglect the personal cleansing is to keep the pollution. What are the promises? Chapter 6 is the answer: "I will dwell in them, and walk in them; and I will be their God, and they shall be my people." "I will be a Father unto you, and ye shall be my sons and daughters." Because of the promise the cleansing command is this: "Touch not the unclean thing; and I will receive you" (vv. 16-18).

It is evident that disciples under the influence of the Father have a definite thing to do. Having put their faith in the promise they must take resolute action towards cleansing from the unclean thing, whatever it is. No half-measures; no secret reservations; no escape routes; no reserves for rebuilding the old bridges in case we need to retreat. The call is for firm, clear-cut action. Associations, habits, friendships, indulgences which are known to lead to impurity must be renounced and denied. Cut the cord, burn every bridge. Go back to the early days, before you got involved in tainted things. Go back to the beginning when the vision was bright and separation entire.

"Flee youthful lusts"

When the King was walking amid the seven golden candlesticks he said to Ephesus: "I have this against thee, that thou didst leave thy first love. Repent and do the first works." It means going back to the things which you once loved and have since neglected. And here is the paradox: as you go back you move forward. The easiest way to fall into sin is to flirt with temptation. The best way to keep away from impurity is to avoid the occasions of impurity. For example and to put it bluntly: if you want to get rid of impure thoughts avoid the impure books. Cleanse the cupboard and you start to cleanse the mind. When Joseph was being enticed by Potiphar's wife, "he fled and got him out". Paul says to Timothy: "Flee youthful lusts". Sometimes to dally means doom.

The second passage to notice is in Matthew 5:13: "Ye are the salt of the earth: but if the salt have lost his savour, wherewith shall it be salted? it is thenceforth good for nothing, but to be cast out and to be trodden under foot of men." The first thing this teaches us is that purity is not just for the perfection of the individual life but that its influence is for the common good. The purpose of salt is to purify, but not to purify itself. Its purpose is to purify the material to which it is applied. It is intended to halt the spread of corruption in the area where it is at work. The influence is altogether antiseptic. Purity in the disciple is like the antiseptic influence of salt. The disciple's purity halts the spread of corruption in the little world where the disciple moves. That point is stressed by the word *earth*. It is not in heaven, nor in the world at large but "Ye are the salt of the earth." The pollution is of the earth, earthy: the standing ground where men corrupt themselves; on the level of the material, in the valley where the dirt collects, where the stench is bad and disease abounds.

The Salt-bearer's Influence

Salt-bearers are not called upon to cleanse the universe, but that limited sphere of influence where every day they move. It is not a crusading march. It is not banner work. It is not with the backing of a great trumpet. The effect of salt is unobtrusive, like leaven in a whole lump: quiet, unseen but real. Disciples become salt because of what they are.

Think what it means in practice. One man or woman in a group lifts the tone of the conversation by their presence. Rudeness, corrupt gossip, mean advantage are restrained and sometimes halted—by a refusal to conform. Homes may not be what they should be: ill-temper, shouted words, slammed doors and the corruption spreads. Hearts are fevered and spirits are unhinged. The home becomes a prison and love is lost, unless some blessed soul is exercised there in the ministry of salt-bearing. Think of recreation. Purity demands that you cannot consent to be amused by things which debase the life of those who amuse you. Neither can you approve recreation which harms your brother or weakens his life in the Truth. The ruin of others is the spread of corruption and purity in discipleship is needed to halt it.

To strive for the purity of salt is a searching quest. It stresses that you cannot exercise salt externally unless you have it internally. Jesus said: "Ye *are* the salt of the earth." It is not an adjunct—it is you. We cannot be pure in public and impure in private. The double life is outlawed. Window dressing will do no good. Mask-wearing is useless. Salt has to be genuine. Perhaps this is what Jesus meant by, "but if the salt have lost his savour, wherewith shall it be salted? it is thenceforth good for nothing". It has happened that disciples remained silent when they should have spoken out for purity, because to have made a stand would have revealed a discrepancy between their known life and the principles they should have defended. Striving for purity is a quest with problems.

This is emphasised by the third passage to ponder in Titus 1:15: "Unto the pure all things are pure; but unto them that are defiled and unbelieving is nothing pure: but even their mind and conscience is defiled." Obviously the Apostle Paul did not mean that things which are impure in themselves will appear pure to the pure in mind. He means that things which are not impure are seen in their purity by the pure in mind. He is stressing this because of the fact to which he is drawing attention: that to those who are themselves *defiled*, nothing is pure. The impure mind sees impurity everywhere. The inflamed imagination turns innocence into guilt and sees disorder where truly there is peace. The world is turned into a wilderness by those with a defiled consciousness.

Thankfully the opposite is true. A man who is seeking to be pure, views others in the light of that purity he himself is seeking. He does not, because his heart is pure, want to see in others the evil he is seeking to avoid in himself. It is a healthy view of the world. It is not blind to the evil, but like love it does not rejoice in it, least of all generate it. A pure mind hopeth all things.

Finally: the probation which leads to purity is part of the evangel of the cross. "How much more shall the blood of Christ . . . cleanse your conscience from dead works to serve the living God?" (Heb. 9:14). Dead works is a reference to the defilement which follows upon contact with the dead under the old law: not by human endeavour, nor by human cleverness is the defilement purged but alone by the mystery of the shed blood. The search for purity is not optional, it is an essential part of the process of redemption. Said Jesus: "Blessed are the pure in heart, for they shall see God."

9

PEACE

IN this case we are not considering the ploughshare, pruninghook peace between nations proclaimed by Isaiah and Micah: more truly that individual heart peace to which the apostle Paul referred when he said, "Let the peace of God rule in your hearts" (Col. 3:15). What we have to consider in this article is the nature of that peace, what it is and what it is not.

Across the meadow from the home of the writer there is a pool. It is a place of peace. No fish ever breaks the surface of the water; no kingfisher ever disturbs the reeds; no water fowl ever calls to its mate; the chatter of moorhens is never heard. Across the surface of that pool there is a thin layer of fine green weed. At this spot peace reigns. It is peace by stagnation. What is the counterpart of this in daily life?

Here is an estimate: a man who is not disturbed by the chances and changes of fortune. He is not rich necessarily but he is comfortable. He is not worried by the market. Tomorrow's bread and next year's holidays give him no cause for concern. He is able to satisfy his desires as they arise. He is never biting his nails about the rent, the mortgage or the bank statement. On the level of day to day needs he is at peace. What are called the cares of life give him no anxiety. He is never upset by controversy because he never bothers to be involved in it. His defence against the spiritual dangers of life is indifference. Ignore them and they will do you no harm. He is not upset by the pains and problems of others because he never notices them. He is never aggravated by his faith being challenged because he never makes it known. So in a certain sense

36

he is at peace—but it is not the peace of God. It is peace by stagnation.

Then there is the peace of inanity: a life lived purely for pleasure. Happiness consists of one thing—the satisfaction of the senses. Repose comes through every desire being gratified. The flesh is made content—the spirit is dead through boredom. The mind is atrophied: the peace of mental torpor. The dead are at peace, we say, and so are some of the living for almost the same reason. The peace of inanity—but very far from the peace of God.

Human Ideas of Peace

There is a kind of peace which in its generation is the very opposite of the foregoing. The writer has observed in some people a remarkable sense of peace secured through spending their whole time *working*. It is often achieved through satisfaction—the satisfaction of drawing near to or reaching a goal; a far-away ambition becoming more possible with every new effort; a spirit that cannot rest if it is compelled for some reason to endure rest.

The pursuit of a cause continually and relentlessly brings a kind of tranquillity. To pause is a reproach. To abandon the work, however briefly, is a disgrace. The only satisfying way to live is to keep working: the peace of toil. Commendable in many ways, but because it is the whole-hearted devotion of life to human ambitions, it cannot be true for the disciple of Christ. Because it is the dedication of human powers to human aims, it cannot be the way of finding the peace of God.

There is a popular idea which has provoked a popular ambition: that one way to peace is to live in the country. The recipe is a cottage, with a honeysuckle door and a rose bordered path. People who believe this have confused peace with quietness. Peace is a condition of the mind; quietness is freedom from noise and interruption. Peace is a permanent condition; quietness is transitory. Only serious things can disturb peace; trivial things disturb quietness.

You can be calm in the city just as well as in the country. You do not need honeysuckle to make you placid. It may be argued that restfulness needs the right circumstances but the truth is, the right circumstances are to be found in the country and in the town. To put it bluntly, country people are as worried, as disturbed and as discomposed as anybody else, given the causes. Obviously there is more tranquillity down a country lane than there is next door to a steel works, but whether there is more peace of the real kind is questionable.

To be fair, we should not underestimate the value of quietness in the right place at the right time. It is a blessed thing, especially in the pursuit of prayer and meditation. What is being stressed is that quietness is a human thing, humanly controlled. By itself it is not a substitute for real peace.

The Peace of God

The peace of God does not depend upon outward circumstances. If it did then men would never have been able to sing in prison or live contentedly with nothing. This peace is as tranquil in January as it is in June. Sunshine or storm, it is constant. As it is not based upon outward circumstances, it cannot be destroyed by them. Its roots are in eternal things, so it cannot be overthrown by transient things.

One proof of this is to recall the circumstances in which the words of Paul were inscribed, quoted in the first paragraph. The Colossian letter was written from Rome where the apostle lay in prison, daily and hourly expecting a violent death. It was written in a time of persecution when false doctrine was rife and religious animosity was fierce. The words about peace were given in the context of the most earnest and eager controversy. So we must notice that according to the apostle Paul it is possible for a disciple to have the peace of God ruling in his heart and yet be at the very point of death; in the very midst of danger; in the very centre of religious controversy and surrounded by bitterness and hatred. We are driven to the conclusion, therefore, that the peace of God is not circumstantial.

Peace Ruling in the Heart

The proposal is that there are three great spiritual factors which create true peace in the heart: (1) that sin and death have been mastered in the Redeemer and that the fruits of his victory are communicated to the disciples. Through pardon and promise and power we have entered into a new life; (2) that all things work together for good to them that love God and are called according to His purpose. That to be where God wants us to be is to be in the best place of all, even though for the time being it may be the place of hardship and difficulty; (3) the best is yet to be. The future has begun but its finest realisation is coming. The vision on the distant boundary is not a mirage—it is the surest sign that God reigneth. The masterpiece of the Gospel—the kingdom of God—is soon to transform the children of God and the world. Nothing can defeat the enthronement of the King. Herein is perfect peace.

Let it not be misunderstood. It does not mean that the disciple is never worried. A disciple ought to be genuinely concerned over things which deserve concern. When the children are sick; when the rent is due; when the roof leaks, anxiety is perfectly proper. This is self-evident. The right perspective is concern without panic; anxiety without despair. Human nature being what it is, sometimes the soul is overwhelmed. It is then that the peace of God is a bulwark. It brings heart peace and soul rest. Like living water it cools the heat and soothes the soreness.

Peace in Action

One of the best examples of these principles in action is to be discerned in a passage from the letter to the Philippians: "Not that I speak in respect of want: for I have learned, in whatsoever state I am, therein to be content. I know how to be abased, and I know also how to abound: in everything and in all things have I learned the secret both to be filled and to be hungry, both to abound and to be in want. I can do all things in him that strengtheneth me" (4:11-13, R.V.).

Whether it was in abundance or in austerity, Paul was at peace. In abundance he was not filled with euphoria, in austerity he was not filled with gloom. He was able to live in the midst of the circumstances, so as to be content with either. One method of dealing with such circumstances is through isolation. Another method is through an attitude of steely fortitude. The Christian method followed by Paul is through use of the circumstances to the best advantage—plenty or penury, to use both and be mastered by neither; good or bad, so to work the will of God that benefit emerges. This was Paul's method, and by it he found contentment. It may seem a contradiction, detachment through use, but in the very contradiction the real truth is discovered.

Be sure that the peace of God does not come overnight. It does

39

not come with a first reading of the Statement of Faith. It begins when the burden of guilt is assuaged. It grows when faith brings humble confidence. It develops when theory is realised through experience. We have a theory that the peace of God passes understanding. We have a witness who testifies that the theory works. The witness says, "Let the peace of God rule in your hearts."

Go back to the honeysuckle. The theory is that it is one of the most fragrant of the English collection. Proof that the theory works is discovered on a June evening in an English garden. That is the moment of truth about the honeysuckle. So it is with the peace of God; notwithstanding the discord between a man's desires and a man's lot; notwithstanding the discrepancy between his aspirations and his achievements; notwithstanding the flux and failure of human life. Never mind the contradictions—peace will rule in the heart if a man will let it.

It cannot be manufactured. It is a divinely natural thing. It comes through a fusion of faith and fidelity. There is one criterion: the more you obey the more it develops. If you disobey, it tends to disappear. Isaiah puts this beyond dispute: "There is no peace, saith my God, to the wicked" (Isa. 57:21).

10

HUMILITY

THIS is a difficult one. Disciples ought to be humble: pride is the very antithesis of discipleship. Yet here is the problem: in striving for humility, the very essence of it can be eroded. Putting it plainly, when you know you are humble it tends to make you proud. It seems, therefore, that humility is not so much a virtue which you can strive for and achieve by itself—it is more the unconscious outcome of other forces operating in a disciple's character. For example, you can on a certain date resolve to be loving all day and when you fall asleep you can say that you have acted lovingly. But somehow to do the same with humility does not bring the same result. Love is active, practical and positive. But with humility you can act humbly without being humble.

Taking the Lowest Place

Put it to the test. Suppose somebody praises you for your service. It may be speaking or writing, teaching or pastoral work. In response to the praise you act humbly—you say it is nothing; it is a poor effort really, not worthy of such notice. This kind of humility you can live with. But suppose somebody else says about your service what you have said yourself. Suppose *they* say it is nothing; it is a poor effort really, not worthy of notice. How do you react then? Do you resent it? Inwardly are you angry? If so, it reveals that your own humble estimate of your service is not as humble as it seems. If it is real humility we should be willing for others to agree with us about the value of what we have done.

A truly humble man is ready for others to treat him in the way he says he deserves. Sometimes in prayer a man may say that the lowest place is good enough for him and when later on he is offered it he takes umbrage and complains about the lack of appreciation in his fellows. Sometimes it happens that our prayers and our hymns make us to be hypocrites. Some people are always ready to take the lowest place if there is somebody else ready to notice it.

The purpose of this argument is to stress that you cannot "do" humility like you can some other virtues. Sometimes you hear people say, "In my humble way I did this or that". When people are conscious of their humility they are on the way to losing it. Sometimes a window is better than a mirror. A man may be as old as he feels but he is never as important. That is why humility is so unnatural. That is why it is so difficult.

Reverence and Awe

The prophet Isaiah reveals that man does have a greatness, and here is the contradiction: it is discovered in a humble and contrite spirit. Man is humble through the realisation of God's greatness. "For thus saith the high and lofty One that inhabiteth eternity, whose name is Holy; I dwell in the high and holy place, with him also that is of a contrite and humble spirit" (57:15). Humility arises from reverence, and reverence is compelled by a realisation of what God is, what He has done in the past, what He is doing now and what He will do ere long. Humility arises from a recognition of the absolute and utter sufficiency of God; a recognition of God's throne in the world and in human life.

It means bowing with awe in the presence of the aweful superiority of God. It comes from a recognition of our absolute dependence upon God. It is a confession that all we need for our life is to be found in the life of God; a surrender to the conviction that we are altogether incomplete, save as we are brought into relationship with Him.

A sense of our need and His wonderful resource provokes meekness. A sense of our predicament and His loving solution compels us to walk humbly before Him, doing justly and loving mercy. Humility is an attitude of subjection out of love for the King's goodness. How can understanding men and women ever be proud in the presence of the God of eternal time, of unlimited space, of unchangeable character—God infinite in grace and matchless in love? It is the knowledge of God which generates the birth of humility in the soul. It is not created by passing resolutions nor by making rules. It is the divinely natural outcome of the knowledge of God—in the mind, in the heart and in experience.

There are men today who rejoice in the beauty of the world around them, investigate it and study it—yet have no reverence for the One who made it. They marvel at the laws of the universe and ignore the Lawgiver. They analyse nature and deny nature's God. They are often nice people, sincere, clever and competent, but they are people with unhumbled hearts. In a sense their file leader is the Pharaoh of Moses' day. He was proud through ignorance—he said it himself: "Who is the Lord that I should obey his voice?"

The Knowledge of Self

The other element at the heart of humility is a right estimate of self, the capacity to see ourselves as God sees us. He knows us through and through. There is no place to hide. We may elude the vigilance of human eyes but who can escape His piercing view? "All things are open and naked to him with whom we have to do." Our brethren see us blunder, but God knows why we do it. Our nature is undone. Sometimes it is galled, jealous and bitter. Too often we are suppliants for human admiration. We respect the things which minister to our comfort and our ambition. Sometimes mean things are exalted in the cause of human advancement. We are dazzled by human glory, delighted to win human approval. The devious complexity of human nature is at the root of the perverted habits of life without God. This is how God sees us standing by ourselves: life emaciated, distorted and spiritually malformed. The point is that when we realise it we ought to be humbled.

Can any person looking at the portrait in Romans 3:9-18 be satisfied with Self? It is a full-length portrait. It begins with "There is none righteous" and ends with "There is no fear of God before their eyes." The first condition is explained by the second. It means there is no humility. When we realise this, we ought to be changed. Think what the change could mean: willing to be anywhere if God wants us there; willing to do anything if God wants us doing it; glad to be silent rather than speak proudly; satisfied to be forgotten if to be remembered feeds our self-esteem; glad to help others do what we might have done ourselves for our reputation's good; anxious to serve for love's sake and not minding how small it may seem; able to do important things without becoming self-important. This is the true meaning of humility.

There is an interesting passage in Galatians 6:1-2 about the restoration of those who have gone wrong: "Brethren, if a man be overtaken in a fault, ye which are spiritual, restore such an one *in the spirit of meekness*; considering thyself, lest thou also be tempted." "In the spirit of meekness" means with true humility. It means that other people's failure ought to make us humble. We ought to be impressed by how fragile we are by ourselves.

Think what failure often is—the result of weakness combined with opportunity; inclination suddenly joined by favourable circumstances. Some people are straight because they lack the chance to be crooked. It means we have no cause to be superior. Have we met the temptation face to face, defied it, overcome it and passed through the ordeal unscathed and triumphant. Or are we intact simply because so far we are untried? So the wisdom of God through Paul says: "Consider thyself, lest thou also be tempted."

In the presence of our brother's failure, anger is no good. It is the argument of lost causes. Censure itself cannot effect restoration. Petulance often deepens the despair. People who carry weight ought not to throw it about. The only solution is love desiring our brother's spiritual good above all else: love expressed in the spirit of meekness. That alone will succeed.

The Humility of True Greatness

We can be sure of one thing. The meekness enjoined upon Christ's disciples is not the meekness of human nature. If it was, Christ has died in vain. In truth it is the meekness of Christ communicated to the disciples. Mark this once more: "Being found in fashion as a man, he humbled himself, and became obedient unto death, even the death of the cross." It was not submission through weakness. It was not resignation through infirmity. Christ did not simply resign himself to God's will—he acquiesced in it. The humble Christ was not passive, he was active—active in opposition to sin, active in the cause of love. The humble Christ was strong with the strength expressed in persistent activity for the purpose of God towards broken humanity. Human strength is often just obstinacy, and obstinacy is the lowest form of determination.

So, measured by the meekness of Christ, humility is not the assumption of a shrinking attitude, pretending that things are not what they are. It is not a prudent calculation to be lowly. It is a love-mastered inclination to serve in small things or great, without thought to renown. Humility is unconscious meekness, too committed to worry about reputation. Of the man who humbled himself it is written: "He took the form of the servant." Love vaunteth not itself. Meekness is love's quality. Let this mind be in you.

11

HOLINESS

THERE are two aspects to holiness, distinct but strongly connected. The first could be called holiness by association. That means that something is holy because of being set apart for the divine purpose. Somebody is holy by reason of being called to some special work for God. The vessels of the temple were holy because of association with the holiness of the altar. The high priest was holy because of his calling and appointment. This is holiness by association.

The second aspect could be called holiness by achievement. It refers to people. Those who are called and appointed, being thereby holy by association, seek to match that condition by a life of active holiness. The first is status, the second is a way of life.

Saints and Saintship

These two aspects can be discerned in the Ephesian letter. In Ephesians 1:1 the Apostle Paul writes to "the saints which are at Ephesus". That is a description of the calling—saintship. A saint is one set apart, sanctified by election—holy by association. In Ephesians 5:3 Paul exhorts the Ephesian believers to live "as becometh saints". It is a call for lives lived in accordance with their status. He is saying: Since you are saints, then live as becometh saints.

That this was the apostle's intention is proved by a clear declaration at the beginning of chapter 4: "I therefore . . . beseech you to walk worthily of the calling wherewith ye were called." The words which follow have to do with personal relationships: husbands, wives, children, parents, masters, servants—responsibilities and personal conduct. In short, the realisation of the holy calling in the experience of daily life. So the main purpose of the letter is to urge a personal and practical application of the meaning of the vocation in such a way as to ensure that these believers should live like saints. This is holiness by achievement.

We need now a more precise definition of holiness. That it is close to righteousness there can be no doubt, but the writer has come to the conclusion that there is a difference between righteousness and holiness. The distinction can be noticed in two passages in the New Testament. The son of Zacharias in Luke 1:74: "to grant unto us that we being delivered out of the hands of our enemies should serve God without fear, in holiness and righteousness before him all our days." Then the apostle Paul exhorts his readers in Ephesus to "put on the new man, which after God hath been created in righteousness and true holiness" (Eph. 4:24).

The particular word translated "holiness" in these two passages occurs nowhere else in the New Testament. It has in it the idea of grace. It has a strong flavour of compassion—a spirit of kindness. The essential ingredient of righteousness and holiness is the same, that is *rightness*, but the difference lies in the sphere of operation. Here is an attempt at a definition. Righteousness is rightness of conduct. Holiness is rightness of character.

It is possible for people to do right things for all kinds of reasons: self-interest, loyalty, pity, self-fulfilment. True righteousness is inspired by holiness, and holiness in the disciple is an approximation to the character of Christ. If it had to be defined in one sentence then it could well be in John 1:17: "For the law was given by Moses: grace and truth came by Jesus Christ." Holiness at its best is a character full of grace and truth. In the genius of discipleship it means being truth-governed and love-impulsed. The question is sometimes asked: How can we know if we have holiness? The answer in all honesty needs to ask another question: How much are we in character people of grace and truth?

Holiness and Fruitfulness

The quest can be pursued in another way. Apply the measurement of Jesus: "By their fruits ye shall know them." Holiness bears fruit. Fruit does not come by magic overnight—it grows. In the realm of growth you are of necessity in the realm of slowness.

47

Furthermore, to some extent it is imperceptible, though the stages are discernible. There is the bud stage, then the blossom stage and then the fruit stage. Each stage is vital and true and in itself represents real achievement. Each stage has a kind of perfection if it encourages the process forward, and onward to the next stage. For example, the bud may be a perfect bud, but if it is still a perfect bud at the blossom stage its perfection has withered. A two year old baby may be a perfect child but if that two year old perfection is still there at say five years, we call it arrested development. Fruit demands growth and growth implies development from within.

How is the fruit recognised? Rather than get involved with some theory of heredity and environment, the writer believes it is better to take a few practical issues and test them honestly in the light of our own personal discipleship. The issues chosen are these: love of self, love of the world, desire for things, love of home and family.

An Honest Self-Examination

The questions to be asked ought to be these:

Love of self: Are we less self-centred today than we were say five years ago? Is our life more God-centred now? Are we glad and willing to serve Christ's cause even though it restricts our self-indulgence and involves some self-denial? Have we more and more put Christ on the throne?

Love of the world: How much do we welcome the admiration of the world, compared with the old days? Do we secretly envy its rank and status? Although in public we despise its glitter, do we in private wish we had more of it? Do we long to get on above all else?

Desire for things: Do we give verbal agreement to the idea that life does not consist in the ownership of things, but then live as though it did? Are we hoping to get more and do better? Insofar as we are able to accumulate wealth, is it more for the purpose of helping others and to advance the cause of Christ?

Love of home and family: Love of these is right and true but Jesus said there may come a time when a disciple has to put his discipleship before home and family. It may never happen to us, but if it did how would we react? Sometimes men for the love of another would do a sinful thing or a mean thing. Would we for love of kindred, perhaps in a crisis, be disloyal to Christ and his cause?

And if we would at one time, would we now? By these kinds of questions, asked and answered honestly, we may be able to discern the development of holiness in our own lives.

Estimated positively we must understand that character is formed out of conduct. If you desire a loving character, then begin to act lovingly. If you want to become trustworthy then be ready to receive and reverence the trust of others. In the end it is never achieved by talking and disputing. To speculate and never to venture is to render the process barren: the blessing of God thwarted by indifference. The way to holiness is by a genuine surrender to the commands of God—will, intellect and emotion. The word achievement may seem boastful. It has to be said that it is not achieved by human endeavour but by the surrender of the life to Christ in order to give him entrance and fellowship. It does involve the renunciation of the evil thing and the repudiation of the forces which hinder and impede.

The writer remembers a story, heard years ago, which illustrates this point. A father and his young son were in Keble College, Oxford, inspecting Holman Hunt's picture 'The Light of the World'—a portrayal of Christ standing and knocking at the shut door. The boy says to his father, "Why do they not open the door?" The father replies, "I do not know son, perhaps they cannot hear the knocking." After a little while the boy says, "I know why they cannot hear the knocking: they are living in the basement." The way to holiness is first to give up living in the basement, amid the low things and base things; then a positive move to the guest room and the open door, because there is fellowship and friendship; there is light and purity; there Christ dwells by faith with his next of kin.

Holiness is God's Will

In the end men become like the God they worship. Those who worship an insensate god become themselves insensate. The principle is true of holiness. In Leviticus 11 there is a comprehensive declaration which is timelessly true: "Ye shall be holy; for I the Lord your God am holy." It is restated in the New Testament in these words: "Ye therefore shall be perfect, as your heavenly Father is perfect." Let us not be dismayed by the absolute nature of the declaration. It is a revelation of the ideal—it is God's thought for man. Man needs the ideal to keep him in the path of endeavour. If he is to strive he must strive upwards. He needs a vision on the boundary to inspire him through the wilderness. Give him the attainable, surround him with the humanly possible and soon he is self-satisfied and boastful.

As disciples, and in the light of the vocation and in response to the exhortation to live as becometh saints, we ought first to ask ourselves about our own particular hindrances. Give them right names. Drag them into the light. Be they friend, habit or indulgence, face them front to front. Bravely be done with them once for all, in the solemn pursuit of holiness. Remember, holiness is the will of God for the saints. "Even as he chose us in him before the foundation of the world, that we should be holy and without blemish before him in love" (Eph. 1:4). Chosen for holiness: "For whom he foreknew, he also foreordained to be conformed to the image of his Son, that he might be the firstborn among many brethren" (Rom. 8:29, R.V.). Foreordained to character: this is holiness, the fulfilment of the high purpose of God's will in those called to be saints.

12

PRAYER

"HOW MUCH MORE SHALL YOUR FATHER . . . ?"

PLACE, posture and persistence are significant aspects of prayer. Frequency and clock time are important. But the writer has come to the conclusion that the one aspect of prayer which disciples are interested in above all else is *purpose*. What exactly is prayer intended to achieve? Put another way, what are the possibilities of prayer?

It may be thought strange that attention is focused so sharply upon something so fundamental. Surely the potential of prayer would have been settled in the early steps of discipleship? Perhaps it ought to be, but the truth is that in practice very often it is not. Sometimes mature disciples are driven to re-think their view of what prayer is supposed to accomplish. The writer has known cases where disciples of long standing changed their view about the purpose of prayer.

The reasons are not always plainly evident, but sometimes with care they can be discerned. For example, perplexity about whether it is right to pray for certain things; the problem of unanswered prayer; the difference between the Biblical experience of prayer and our experience today. Then, in the view of some disciples, there seem to be so many contradictions. The weak seem to pray well and yet it taxes the strength of the strong. It is clear and straightforward and yet sometimes it is full of mystery. Some praying leaves us cold and empty. Again, with some, the gap between praying and actual living results in a reluctance to pray. Some hear about communion in prayer but never really find it. Another thing: words run out so quickly. Jesus spent nights in prayer—we are finished in five minutes. Some tell of wonderful prayer blessings but others, by contrast, say they come away bereft.

These are some of the reasons why disciples ask about the purpose of prayer. They are certain it is a great privilege to pray, but sometimes they are uncertain about its possibilities.

Two Pathways to Prayer

In the main the attitudes of disciples towards prayer can be divided into two categories: firstly, those who believe that prayer has both objective and subjective values; secondly, those who believe that prayer has a subjective value only. Think of the first category more precisely. It means that prayer can change things outside of ourselves as well as changing us internally. It is a conviction that God will overrule His own laws for our sakes, if it is in harmony with His will. It is faith that God hears and grants the requests of those who pray, sometimes changing circumstances and altering conditions. It recognises that the subjective value of prayer arises out of faith in its objective value.

If disciples ask and receive, their faith is strengthened. If they ask and receive an unexpected answer, they are disciplined. When they knock and the door is opened, their gratitude is deepened. If they seek, they find their resolution is fortified. When disciples are convinced that their prayers are heard and answered, they tend to pray more, not less.

Think of the second category—that prayer is subjective only. Those who hold this view believe sincerely that prayer is good and essential because it changes those who pray. Drawing near in worship, thankfulness and praise is a great privilege and should not be under-valued. To ask God to change the laws of the universe for our sakes is mistaken and could well result in disappointment and despair.

We have to face the fact that believers are subject to the chances and changes of life as are other people, and nothing can alter this. The right approach is to ask God to give us strength to understand and endure life, not to change it. God does not temper the wind to the shorn lamb, but he will give the lamb a good thick coat to stand against it.

It is argued that when people pray objectively, asking for things, it is usually for something they want keenly, even desperately. If they get what they want it is probably because they have striven for it themselves. It is said that what you pray for you work for; the age of miracles is closed. The right thing is to pray for guidance through the Word of God; to seek for strength and wisdom through the experience of fellowship; to ask that through adversity and trial we may find strength and resolution. Prayer is vital because man needs to communicate with his Creator. Thereby the spirit is purified and empowered.

Both categories have their problems. In the first, strong expectations are always exposed to the possibility of strong frustration. If you look for great things you may be disappointed. In old time they prayed and the answer was clear and uninterrupted. Today it is not like that. The answer is sometimes difficult to recognise. What to one person is an answer is to another without significance. What to one is exceptional is to another ordinary. Today there is no voice, no fire, no thunder. Blessings which come to those who pray seem also to come to those who do not. Questions arise: Would it have happened anyway? Do we expect too much?

The Problem of a Plea Refused

The writer remembers something from long ago, in the young days when we were spiritually simple. Our sister was seriously ill. She was good and faithful and true. We prayed, confidently, trustingly, persistently. She recovered wonderfully. We rejoiced and thanked God. Then almost in the midst of our thanksgiving she collapsed and died. The shock was almost unbearable. The landscape was suddenly dark and desolate. The blue sky was iron grey and seemed impenetrable. We looked on the corpse and knew that God had refused our plea. Our spirits were shattered and our faith was tried with fire. There and then it proved one thing—that the petitions of earnest, sincere disciples, offered in faith, are not always granted. Notwithstanding objective prayer, enemies seem to triumph, sickness abounds, apathy invades the spirit and misfortune sometimes overwhelms the saints.

Another problem connected with objective prayer is that other religious people who do not have the Truth, testify confidently about their experience of answered prayer. The evidence they cite as proof is exactly that experienced by the saints. They refer to the same kind of praying and the same kind of results. This tends to make those in the second category doubt the evidence altogether. It tends to make them suspicious about the soundness of the objective prayer theory.

Hannah's Persistence

The subjective theory has its difficulties too. In the main they are twofold. First of all the discrepancy between praying in Bible times and praying today, according to their view of it. Does it mean we have to face the fact that God's attitude to prayer has changed? There can be no doubt that in Bible times God definitely responded to objective prayer. For example, it would have been no good trying to explain to Hannah the subjective-only theory. It would have been a waste of time trying to convince her that the laws of nature cannot be changed. She believed that somehow the God of Israel was in charge of the laws He had made. She could not accept that He was a prisoner in His own purpose. Hannah wanted a child. Her heart yearned in sorrow for a son. Anguish of soul is not impressed by rules and regulations. With this kind of persistence nothing is final. Hannah prayed objectively and God answered with Samuel.

Asa's Boldness

Another example: Asa found himself amid circumstances beyond his power to control. Suddenly he was confronted by Zerah and a million men bent upon the destruction of Judah. Defeat was inevitable. When the need is urgent, there is no time for bush beating. Asa turned to God in one of the boldest prayers in the Bible (2 Chron. 14:11). In effect he placed the burden of survival squarely with God. What he said amounted to this: "If we fail Lord, it will be your failure." Somehow Asa thought he could enlist the supernatural and he was proved right. The victory for Judah was splendid and complete.

Hezekiah . . . Paul

Again, Hezekiah asked very objectively, and the decision made by God was changed by God. Fifteen years of extra life to a man who was under the sentence of death is a very substantial answer. Whether it was wise is not our business. Another example: Paul prayed objectively for the removal of his disability. The answer when it came was not the one he expected, but that does not prove his praying was wrong. Paul believed that God could relieve the pain and God did, even more deeply than Paul ever imagined. The problem is that if these things were right then, why are they wrong now?

The second problem under this category is the distinct possibility that where disciples believe that prayer is not answered objectively they will be tempted to give up praying. This is especially true in desperate circumstances when an objective answer would be a Godsend. Nothing encourages prayer more than faith that it is heard and answered. Nothing discourages prayer more than the idea that it really makes no difference in the end.

Decisive Evidence

To the writer it seems that the possibilities of prayer have to be measured by a consideration of three pieces of evidence: First of all, our understanding of the Fatherhood of God. It is not a figure of speech. We believe with all our heart that He is our Father in the truest sense. It is no accident that the best prayer of all begins with "Our Father". Every faithful father knows what fatherhood means: doing the best in every way for the good of the children. Jesus expressed it powerfully: "If ye then, being evil, know how to give good gifts unto your children, how much more shall your Father in heaven give good things to them that ask him?" (Matt. 7:11). The words that really tell are "how much more". This throws light on the wonderful possibilities.

Then next, the teaching of Jesus. He was categoric. "Ask, and it shall be given you; seek, and ye shall find; knock, and it shall be opened unto you" (Matt. 7:7). Now if we ask and do not receive, if we seek and never find, if we knock and it is not opened, then we feel that somehow the truest man that ever lived has in some way deceived us.

Then thirdly, the experience of the saints—the testimony of praying disciples in every age. They say that the words of Jesus have been vindicated. They did receive; their seeking was not in vain; the door was opened. Can it all be a great mistake? Or was it just dispensational? Was it something to wonder at from a distance?

Having a clear mind about *purpose* is not always easy. We continue the consideration in the next chapter.

55

13

PRAYER

"TO PRAY AND NOT TO FAINT"

MANY disciples believe that the subjective value of prayer arises mainly from a conviction about its objective value. If a man asks God for help and help comes, then faith is increased and the man's resolution to serve and obey is strengthened. Furthermore, it is argued, how can so much spiritual benefit be generated by a theory which is false? In other words, is not the subjective value of prayer presumptive evidence for the truth of its objective value? They say, because disciples are uplifted and ennobled through trusting in the objective power of prayer, the theory must be true and the practice must be good. It could not be that so much good has come out of something which is theologically false. So, the real benefit of prayer arises from trusting in its objective value.

A passage which bears powerfully upon this issue is in Luke 18: "And he spake a parable unto them, to this end, that men ought always to pray and not to faint." Notice the word *men*, because in the Revised Version it is given as *they*. This is not hair splitting: it is important. To some extent the word "men" seems to detach the passage from the context, whereas "they" seems to fit it securely where it ought to be. Notice Jesus spake the parable unto *them*. The identity of "them" is discovered in Luke 17:22: "And he said unto the disciples . . . "

Then there follow solemn words about the hardship and difficulty which they will have to face in seeking to keep true to their calling. He says that if they would keep their life they will have to lose it. He enforces his warning by reminding them of the days of Noah and the days of Lot, and tells them in effect that their experience

56

will be similar. They will have to face stress and strain in holding fast to the faith. Indeed, later on he will tell them of a day when men's hearts will faint for fear when they see awful things coming upon Jerusalem. And therefore he spake a parable unto them, to this end, that *they* ought always to pray and not to faint.

Think what fainting means. The dictionary says that to faint is to become weak, to be feeble, without strength—to lose courage, to give way. In the Bible it has to do with weariness, for Paul says, "Be not weary in well doing: for in due season we shall reap, if we faint not" (Gal. 6:9). It looks as though not to be weary is not to faint. We must understand what weariness is. It is not tiredness. Tiredness is a blessed thing which comes from working and which makes us rest so that we are restored and ready to work again.

But weariness is different—it is not a blessing but a curse. It is losing heart. It is a feeling that things are not worth doing. It means beginning each task with a sigh instead of a smile. It is being dispirited, without motivation. It is losing hope. The words of Isaiah can help us to understand fainting: "Even the youths shall faint and be weary, and the young men shall utterly fall" (Isa. 40:30). The young men represent the strongest and most virile force in the nation—those most likely to keep the city, to hold fast and remain true. Even these shall fail and their awful failure is described in these words: fainting and weariness.

On the other hand, mark those who triumph, for the contrast is a revelation: "They that wait upon the Lord shall renew their strength; they shall mount up with wings as eagles; they shall run, and not be weary; they shall walk and not faint" (v. 31). Here is a definition by contrast: to faint is to be without eagle wings; not to run, not even to walk. In Bible terms it is an awful disability; a paralysis leading to impotence; withered by weakness and wasted by weariness.

The Alternative is Prayer

Jesus says that if disciples desire to avoid fainting they must pray. He does not seem to admit of any middle position. It is one thing or the other. If men pray they will not faint and if they do faint it will be because they have ceased to pray. Notice Jesus says they ought to pray. In this case ought means must. It is a privilege to pray but he is stressing that it is also a duty.

The Apostle Peter once said: "We ought to obey God rather than men" (Acts 5:29). In the Revised Version Peter says: "We *must* obey God rather than men." To some minds the word "ought" suggests something we can do if we like, in order to effect an improvement. It is permissive, not categoric. But Peter meant that there was no alternative—we *must*. So it is in Luke 18: we ought to pray means we must pray. Disciples who are weary and dissatisfied with their spiritual progress, must scrutinise their habit of prayer. If the spirit is low and life in the Truth seems barren—think carefully about the practice of prayer.

Test your methods honestly. You may have to say that yesterday you were too busy with ecclesial work to have time to pray. Last week you were so over-burdened with the cares of this life that prayer was crowded out. When you pray, mostly it is at the meeting or when you give thanks. The actual practice is, perhaps, two minutes of "lay me down to sleep" prayer. If the reader thinks he detects that the writer is speaking out of experience, the reader is right. The King's words are true: disciples get nearer to fainting when they get away from praying.

The True Value of Prayer

Prayer has been defined as the raising of the heart and mind to God; the soul's sincere desire, uttered or unexpressed; communion with heaven. It includes worship and praise; it provides for petition and entreaty. Disciples may ask and hope to receive; they knock and the door is opened. But it goes even further than this. As prayer stands in opposition to fainting, it stands also for the opposite of all the things which fainting represents.

By this method we may discern the real subjective value of prayer. If fainting means the dimming of the vision, then prayer is seeing the distant boundary in bright clearness, horizoned by faith. If fainting means to feel life ebbing away, then prayer is to be conscious of life becoming full and free and faithful. If fainting is weakness, then prayer is strength. If fainting is to be weary and without vigour, then prayer is confidence and inspiration. Measured by Isaiah, prayer is mounting up with eagle wings; it is running and not being weary; it is walking and not fainting. Instead of disappointment, joy; instead of fear, tranquillity; instead of anxiety, peace.

These blessed qualities in the subjective value of prayer are provoked by the conviction that God the Father answers the prayers of His children. They seek, and because of His providence, they find. Think of the parable in Luke 18. It is a parable of contrasts. All that the unjust judge was, God is not. The judge was indifferent; he did not care for anybody. He was interested only in himself. His character is summed up in one word: he was unrighteous. By contrast God is righteous. He careth for you. He is longsuffering and will do justice to his elect speedily.

The judge responded at last only because it suited his selfish purposes. He did not want to help the widow—he wanted to be rid of her. By contrast God responds for our sakes. He grants those things which will bless and denies those things which will harm. His motive is love. The judge responded at last because of the widow's importunity. He acted because he was weary of her continual coming. He hated her persistence. God is not like this. Our praying is not the importunity of the widow. If disciples are doing what Jesus commands—always praying—there is no need to talk of importunity.

Prayer life is always Godward and therefore it is regular and rightly habitual. The response of God according to the parable is willing, ready and compassionate. The divine answer may have to be no, but it is not capriciously delayed. If there is a time of waiting it must have a loving purpose, to do good and not to hurt. The parable teaches us that the frailest and the weakest cry is heard in heaven. The judge was fed up. God is never that: He is full of compassion, longsuffering and patient with His children. He is to them what He is declared to be: a Father. The judge was never this.

The Discipline of Prayer

Another way in which the subjective value of prayer is produced is through discipline. To some extent, how we pray affects how we live. It is not that easy to pray in one way, then blatantly to live in another. In some cases the embarrassment is relieved by ceasing to pray, but more often the sincere disciple endeavours to live more nearly as he prays. To some extent the prayers we pray fix a pattern to which we strive to conform. In this way praying is a form of discipline. For example, if you ask God to help you to understand His Word better, you are compelled, in all honesty, to read and study it. That sort of prayer should send you to the Bible Class. How can an honest disciple pray that prayer and then let the Bible get dusty or be absent from opportunities to study it?

If you ask God to bless the needy and comfort those who are lonely and isolated, you are compelled to take some action, where you can. How can an honest disciple pray that prayer and then neglect opportunities to bring succour and help to those in need? If you ask God to bless and strengthen the ecclesia you are compelled to do your best to support it in every way—by your regular presence, your service and your gifts. How can an honest disciple pray that prayer and then be culpably absent or selfishly unwilling to serve or give? The truth is that some kinds of prayer tend to make us hypocrites and for praying disciples hypocrisy is hard to bear. So how we pray affects how we live.

Prayer is for Every Believer

There are some aspects of the religious life which are not available to us for one reason or another. The impediments are varied—our physical condition, our age, our sex, our geographical position, our disabilities, our career, our home life. But there is no barrier to prayer. Every disciple is free to pray: the youngest and the oldest, the weakest and the strongest, the leaders and the led—they ought always to pray and not to faint.

14

PERSPECTIVE

IT could have been loyalty or allegiance, but in the end we settled for perspective. It describes more comprehensively that balance which has to be struck between the claims of the Truth, on the one hand, and on the other the demands which modern life makes upon our time, our substance and our energy. This is an essential part of discipleship. Striking the balance is not optional. Disciples cannot withdraw from the necessity to come to a decision. Standing still is an expression of perspective. Whether we like it or not we have to face the fact that there are some good things which are in competition with the Truth. How we react to this problem is regulated to some extent by the place the Truth occupies in our list of priorities.

The theory is that the Truth has top priority—but every disciple knows that the practice is somewhat different. The theory is that we are living above the snowline, where the air is pure, the vision is clear and the spirit is exhilarated. The practice is that more likely we are living in the valley, where the atmosphere is sometimes murky, the children are sick, the bank manager is not as friendly as he is made out to be and too often we are tired and frustrated. These are the circumstances where we have to get things into perspective.

The Issues are Personal

This is a subject where vague generalities are of little help. To tell the truth, the writer is weary of vague generalities. Giving mental assent to high principles does not really settle the issue of perspective. Of course, we are all against sin. We are all in favour of

61

righteousness. We all believe that the Truth is the most important thing in our lives. With these general statements no one would disagree. It is when things become personal that they become real. If a speaker tells an audience that they are all sinners, no one is offended and nobody turns a hair. But if he goes to one person and accuses him of a sin and tells of the time and place, the reaction is very different. When things move from the general to the particular, they suddenly become real. So it is with this subject. To be of any use we have to leave the vague generalities and get down to what in modern parlance is called the "nitty-gritty".

When we think of giving the Truth top priority there is a strong tendency to think of the great issues of life: some crisis perhaps, where we have to stand up and be counted; some great travail, where out of the agony of conflict we stand firm for the Truth and take the consequences. The writer is compelled to say that if we are looking for this kind of opportunity to give the Truth top priority, we shall wait for half a life-time. He has been in the Truth for nearly forty-four years and in that time twice only has he had to stand up for some great issue and be counted. Twice only has he had to give the Truth top priority and take the consequences. Read the New Testament carefully and it becomes evident that the claims of the Truth have to be met in the commonplace things of life—the infinitesimals of daily living. The forces which are sometimes in competition with the Truth arise out of the things of the home, careers and employment, recreation and leisure. Think of these sentences:

"Husbands, love your wives, as Christ also loved the church."

"Wives, submit yourselves unto your own husbands."

"Let them first learn to show piety at home."

"Exhort servants to be in subjection to their own masters."

"Masters, forbear threatening, knowing that their master and yours is in heaven."

"Children, obey your parents in all things."

"See that ye abound in this grace also" ("this grace" here is the giving of money).

"The grace of God hath appeared, bringing salvation to all men and instructing us, to the intent that, denying ungodliness and worldly lusts, we should live soberly, righteously and godly . . ."

So perspective is not something postponed to the day of the earthquake or the final battle. The balance has to be struck every day. By this measurement the claims of the Truth are recognised in our service to the ecclesia and our relationship with other members of the ecclesial family. This is something which is realised every day, every week and through every year. The question which has constantly to be faced is about the kind of priority we are willing to give to these things: not just in theory but in practice.

Just as an example, take the matter of support for the ecclesial meetings: what are we prepared to allow to interfere with our attendance? Or think of service in the work of the ecclesia: at what point do we consider we are entitled to resign the service? Or in our relationship with God's other children: what limitations do we put upon our compassion and care? Or in the grace of giving: what is our conception of generosity? It is precisely in these things that perspective is so important.

Theory and Practice

Getting things into the right perspective is not easy, although in theory it seems easy. The theory is that we should always put the Truth first. In practical terms, the daily, weekly claims of the Truth have to take their place with a dozen other things which demand our time, our substance and our energy. There are times when the things of the home and of employment have to take precedence over some things in the Truth. Whether the things to do with recreation and leisure ought to have priority over the things of the Truth is another matter. Some would say Yes—sometimes; others would say No—never. The situation becomes sad when, having to face the choice, the decision is *always* in favour of the home, the family, the career. In these circumstances the Truth gets the favour only when there is nothing else in competition with it.

Let us not get it wrong. This is not a case of somebody neglecting the claims of the ecclesia when, without impediment, they could easily serve or easily go or easily give. That is a different problem. This is the case of a disciple who, finding the claims of the ecclesia in *competition* with the claims of temporal life, declares that the Truth must take second place. As a result, the place is empty, the work undone, the gift is cancelled.

Sanctified common sense teaches us that there are occasions

when the claims of temporal life must come first at this level: for example, sickness, the solemn duties of home life, the committed contract of employment, the doctor's advice, the command to owe no man anything. These things are important and cannot be neglected. But life is hardly ever black or white. So often it is in between, and the conflicts and competition between the temporal and the spiritual can often be resolved if the disciple is ready to take trouble and care. It may mean being inconvenienced; it may mean getting very tired; it may mean giving up some pleasure or some leisure; it may mean losing some temporal advantage. This is where the right perspective could lead to the very best result—for the disciple and for the Master.

The Proper Balance

The idea of striking a balance suggests a sensible middle course where both sides are evenly positioned: a reasonable allocation to both claims; a judicious moderation, free from ill-balanced extremes. Before we settle happily for this conclusion we ought to examine the teaching of Jesus in Matthew 12. The King casts out a demon and is charged with doing it by the power of Beelzebub. He points out logically that if Satan's kingdom is divided against itself it will perish. Then he adds these significant words: "He that is not with me is against me; and he that gathereth not with me scattereth abroad" (v. 30). We should ponder these words carefully because here we have something important about perspective. Jesus does not seem to be making any provision for a comfortable middle position. There is no place for being neutral. He says that if you are not actually gathering with him you are by your detachment actually scattering. We must not make these words more severe than they are but, on the other hand, we must not treat them casually. It would be quite wrong to say that every disciple who strikes a balance in favour of the temporal is a scatterer. But we must say that every disciple who strikes that kind of balance ought to consider the perspective which Christ reveals. The only way not to be in danger of scattering is always to ensure that we are strongly in favour of gathering.

This declaration of Christ reveals that the true balance is not in the neat middle position, equal to both sides. It is telling us that the balance ought to be heavily weighted in favour of Christ and his cause. This inequality in his favour is by the measurement of heaven truly in balance. It means, in practice, that in the clear shining of two ways the genius of discipleship should lead us to be heavily biased on the side of the Truth, even though it may mean inconvenience, difficulty and even hardship. If this seems outrageous, the reader should understand that getting perspective right can be a painful process. It may mean looking critically at the importance we give to our careers, our families, our homes, our friends and our leisure.

But when all is said and done, the true motive for getting things into the right perspective is not fear or dread or blind compulsion. It is the master principle of love. People give the Truth top priority because they love it. Any other motive will fail and eventually the disciple becomes disgruntled and half-hearted. But when they are love-impulsed, and inspired by what the King has done for our sakes, they favour his cause gladly, happy to be his bond-servants and heavily weighted in his favour. They are not dragging themselves after him, resentful and lukewarm. They follow him with joy and give him their allegiance in the everyday things of the Truth without demur. Loyal for love's sake: this is the true perspective.

15

INDIVIDUALITY

BEGIN with a paradox. All true disciples are seeking to become like the one Master. Yet even in the conformity to the blessed pattern of their Lord, their essential individuality is retained. As they succeed they become alike, and yet their distinct identities are unimpaired. Their characters co-ordinate but their disparate characteristics remain. This is not just a theory, it is proven by observation. Peter and Paul are both loving, faithful and true, but Peter is not Paul and Paul is not Peter. It is part of the genius of discipleship, that in the midst of its sanctified unity, individuality remains. But here is the real issue: the paradox becomes a problem. How far in the unity of the faith ought individuality to be exercised?

Each Disciple is Unique

The first thing to remember is that each disciple has a direct individual relationship with God the Father. As John says, not of the will of the flesh, nor by the will of man, but of God. Alongside the corporate fellowship of the ecclesia, each person stands alone. The calling marks off each individual from other individuals. So we ought not to be surprised to read that every man shall give an account of *himself* to God. There are many things we can do to help our fellow pilgrims on the pilgrim way, but in the end we are measured as independent individuals. It is fair because this is what we are. It is a mystery, but every man is a unique personality. Let us not get it wrong—people are alike in many respects and the differences may be but partial, but they are nevertheless definite.

This means that there are capacities, potentialities and peculiarities that make you uniquely what you are. Among others, this fact is recognised in Proverbs 22:6: "Train up a child in the way he should go, and even when he is old he will not depart from it." In the Revised Version margin it is slightly different and in the opinion of the writer, significantly different: "Train up a child *according to his way* and even when he is old he will not depart from it." The inference is that you cannot treat children all in the same way because every child is different. The words "according to his way" is a recognition of this. In the end the things they have to learn are the same for everyone, but the emphasis and the method and the pressure must vary with the child's temperament.

Most parents have learned this in the developing experience of parenthood. How often has it been confessed: "We have five, and every one is different." The numbers may vary but the fact remains. Perhaps one is sanguine, never to be suppressed. Another tends to be despondent, needing constant encouragement. Another is sceptical, always asking questions, and needing endless patience. Another is credulous and must be warned about the sharpness of life. Another seems to be naturally irreligious and needs strong guidance and careful guarding. Each one is an individual and each one needs to be trained according to his way, as the wise man indicated. It has been said that to instruct is to build in and to educate is to draw out. To do this successfully you must know what the child is, because each is an individual.

The Limitation of Liberty

The same truth is discerned in the New Testament about adults. "Let us consider one another to provoke unto love and good works" (Heb. 10:24). In the New English Bible it goes: "We ought to see how each of us may best arouse others to love and active goodness"; a recognition that different people need different treatment, because they are different.

Anybody with a bit of ecclesial experience knows this to be true. If you are in doubt ask any level-headed recording brother. Some like it blunt, can take it and thrive on it. Others cannot, and that kind of treatment is like walking over their feelings in hob-nail boots. Some are pugnacious and strong, others are retiring and nervous. Some are always confident and others are always feeling their way. Some are steely and others are sentimental. Some find faith easy, others are always seeking reassurance. Some are readily satisfied, others always have problems. Some are like Peter, some are like Thomas, some are like Paul—all want to be like Christ at last. It teaches us that individuality in religion is a fact that has to be faced. It can be a blessing and something to rejoice in but it does present problems. Be careful to understand this rightly. The exercise of individuality gives no right to dispute or be disloyal to the fundamental articles of the faith. To these things we have pledged our hearts and minds gladly. Here there is no provision to dissemble or disprofess.

Individuality is not a cover for those who profess to believe something they do not believe. Nor is it a device to enable false teaching to spread imperceptibly like leaven. For that condition there is a harder word with harder consequences. No—this area of individuality should not provide any opportunities to undermine the unity of the faith. But there are other levels where individual forces rightly can be exercised: insights, ideas, talents, gifts, means, methods in faithful diversity used in the service of the Truth, without harming the proper uniformity. But even in this rightful exercise of individuality, there are responsibilities to be observed.

We Cannot Live for Ourselves Alone

The ecclesia is not a group of individuals who live alone. The units are part of the unity. The ecclesia is an inter-relationship of believing souls. The genius of discipleship cannot flourish in an isolated life. It needs others to complete the circuit. It is one thing to believe in the principle of love, but to be real it needs a loving relationship with others. That is why the ecclesia is called a family and a commonwealth. The Apostle Paul teaches us that if one member suffers, the tremor is felt through all the members; if one member rejoices, the ripple spreads to every heart (1 Cor. 12:26). So it is evident that the individual relationship which a disciple has with God is not just for himself, alone. It has also to do with that individual disciple fitting into the corporate body of believers.

It follows, consequently, that legitimate individuality in the faith must have limitations. We cannot exercise our individuality if in the doing of it our brother is hindered or harmed. Without going into details Romans 14 is the measurement. Paul says that no man liveth to himself and no man dieth to himself. He argues that one of the great objectives of discipleship is to edify one another. He urges us to be very careful about judging one another. That does not mean that we must never reach a judgment but it does mean that we should not condemn others for their peculiarities. Of course, we all agree to this in principle, but it is honoured more in principle than in practice. If Romans 14 is put into practice it means we should judge ourselves *in the interests of our brethren*. Our choices, our words, our reactions, our tempers, our private deeds—are we through our individuality, expressed in these things, helping or hindering our brother for whom Christ died?

The Unlawful Use of Lawful Things

Another saying which is significant in the matter of individuality is in 1 Corinthians. First, the Apostle Paul says: "All things are lawful for me; but not all things are expedient. All things are lawful for me; but I will not be brought under the power of any" (6:12). Then: "All things are lawful; but all things are not expedient. All things are lawful but all things edify not" (10:23). The expression "all things are lawful" makes full provision for the exercise of individuality. The word lawful has to do with the king's highway. It is the opposite of being confined, being imprisoned. It is the freedom to make headway, by any method you may lawfully choose.

But then the Apostle enters a limitation, "but not all things are expedient". Sadly the word expedient has been de-valued. Today it has come to mean something which is profitable without too much reference to principle. But in its first intention it too has to do with the king's highway. It refers to the liberty to advance along the road. (Notice in the centre of the word the syllable *ped* and then think that a pedal is a lever operated by the foot; a pedestrian is a foot traveller and a pedometer is an instrument for measuring the distance traversed by walkers.) "Not all things are expedient" means not all things help the journey forward; not all things give wings to the pilgrim's feet. So when it comes to the exercise of our individuality we have to apply the test of personal progress on the pilgrim way—ours and others': does it help us forward or hold us back?

Then the Apostle says: "I will not be brought under the power of

69

any." It means that the exercise of individuality might be dangerous. It means that a disciple must not be mastered by the lawful things which he allows and enjoys. The liberty to use anything ceases when it enslaves. Keep the right perspective and you are safe; give it priority and you are in danger. The innocent thing is no longer innocent if you cannot control it. So in the exercise of individuality we have to apply the test of mastership.

Then the Apostle says: "Not all things edify." Notice the resemblance between edify and edifice. An edifice is a building and to edify means to build up. This has to some extent been dealt with in the previous paragraph, but there is something to add. Notice that the act of building up is a positive act. It is not something quiescent and neutral. The writer is ready to make a confession. More than once in the use of some hobby or leisure, in the exercise of his own individuality, he has said that this thing does nobody any harm, therefore it is lawful. He wonders now if this is good enough. Ought he rather to have said, Does this thing do anybody any good? He is still uncertain and is always looking for reasons to make his individuality plausible. So as we cannot live alone, we must in the exercise of our individuality apply the test of brotherly relationship.

To attempt a summation, individuality in the faith rightly understood is a blessed thing and brings proper diversity to the work of the ecclesia, variety in the talents of those called to be saints and proper recreation for bodies and minds. But it brings solemn responsibilities. We must notice the breadth and narrowness of its operation. Most of all, in the exercise of the proper limitation of our individual liberty we may find the freedom wherewith Christ has made us free.

16

JOY

DOES the reader recognise this situation? Something is lost at home. Let us say it is an envelope and the contents are important. Everybody says it should be in a certain place but it is not found there. The search goes on throughout the house, without success. Then at last it is found—in the very place where it was supposed to be at first. It had been passed over a dozen times, unrecognised. It was unrecognised because the searcher had a wrong idea of the envelope's shape and colour. For the time being he had forgotten what it really was like, and so it was undiscovered. This is a parable.

One of the criticisms sometimes levelled against us is that as a community we lack joy. But it could well be that joy is there but it is undiscovered because it is unrecognised. That is to say, the critic has a wrong idea of what he is looking for. It may be that he has confused cheerfulness with joy. He says that our services are formal; our hymns are dull; our methods are perfunctory, and therefore there is no joy.

We contend that people can have joy without shouting, dancing or falling about. Let us not make a mistake here. There is nothing wrong with cheerfulness—at home or in the ecclesia. The writer has to confess that he prefers the person who comes to cheer him up rather than the one who comes to read him the Riot Act. Under the right conditions cheerfulness is excellent, but it is not the same as joy. Understand also that sometimes joy is expressed in songs and dance and radiant faces. But if these are absent we must not conclude that joy has gone. Joy may be expressed in the ordinary and

71

the orthodox. David danced and so did Habakkuk; Mary sang a great song; the Emmaus disciples went back at the double and Hannah went home with a lilt in her step.

Let us anticipate a question. Did not Jesus say, "Be of good cheer"? The answer is that he said it five times, always to people in some form of trouble: to the palsied man who was let down through the roof; to the disciples in peril on the sea; to the woman with an issue of blood; to the disciples about to lose their Master; to Paul in prison at Jerusalem. Their troubles were different but to each came the same answer: "Be of good cheer." We can be sure of one thing: the King was not telling them to cheer up. To suffering troubled people that is but a short expedient. The benefit lasts for an hour and then the old sorrow returns.

This was not the Lord's method. Turn up your Bible dictionaries to see what he really said. "Be of good *courage*" was his word of consolation. This call to courage was not just a piece of advice, empty of reason. The reason for the courage was discovered in the fact of Christ himself; what he was doing and would do for them, now and hereafter. To the palsied man, pardon and healing. To the broken woman, comfort and relief. To the frightened sailors, "It is I, be not afraid". To the perplexed disciples, having to face the world, "Be of good courage, I have overcome the world". To the apostle in prison, confined and frustrated, a promise that he would be free and would testify at Rome. In every case it was because of Christ and his power that they were urged to have courage.

Joy at the Last

Our purpose is to stress that cheerfulness is good, but *it is circumstantial*. Cheerfulness exists when conditions are favourable, but when conditions are the opposite, cheerfulness is absent and indeed would be inappropriate. That is why Christ did not tell the troubled, suffering folk to cheer up—and why he did urge them, in the midst of their trouble, to have courage, because in that direction they would at last realise joy. When the heart is heavy, and the spirit is sad and the shadows are long, then cheerfulness, good as it is, will not be possible. The mystery is this—that where cheerfulness is impossible, joy remains. The proposal is that joy transcends adverse circumstances and may even transform them. Remember Paul's words: "As sorrowful, yet alway rejoicing" (2 Cor. 6:10).

Following the suggestiveness of the proposal, think of Acts 16. Two men are in prison. Their backs are torn and lacerated. They are chained in the lowest and darkest dungeon, cramped in the stocks—*and they are singing*. We can be sure they are exercising their discipleship on the highest level. They are not singing just to keep their spirits up; they are singing for joy. The song was the outcome of their gladness. It was the song of the resurrection. The stocks hurt them; their bloody backs pained them, but for some reason they were impelled to offer praise to God. Somehow the joy in their hearts had to find expression in the song, and no pain could muzzle it. The other prisoners heard it because no bars could fetter it.

Rejoicing in Tribulation

Later on one of these men will write some strange and wonderful words: "Let us rejoice in our tribulations, for tribulation worketh patience." Somehow the affliction was being used for good. The foe becomes an ally. This is why, perhaps, one day he will write to the Corinthians: "I overflow with joy in all my afflictions." Or again: "Our light affliction worketh for us a far more exceeding . . . "

The adversity is transmuted into the force of victory. Surely the soul of man shrinks from tribulation? Surely pain brings grief? If and when these things have to be faced, men steel themselves and with stoic fatalism endure the pain and bow to the adversity. Let us not tone it down. It is brave and heroic how people submit to tribulation. They say: "What cannot be cured must be endured." This was the philosophy of stoic paganism but it is not the philosophy of Paul, the servant of Christ.

Out of his own experience he teaches us that in some mysterious way the adversity is part of the cure: that out of the very weakness, the strength of God will be made perfect. In the hand of the Lord there is healing in the very tribulation. That is why joy is possible in circumstances where cheerfulness would fly away. These men were in the dark, but the darkness did not matter because they are children of light. These men were in prison, but the prison did not matter because at the same time they were in Christ.

Do not draw a wrong conclusion. It does not mean that we cannot have joy unless we have suffering. That is false; but it does mean that when suffering comes, joy can remain and be intensified. The King once said to his own: "Your sorrow shall be turned into joy." It is not simply that one condition is exchanged for another, but that the very sorrow itself in some way has a background of joy. Of the suffering Saviour it was written: "Who for the joy set before him endured the cross, despising the shame." We should be wrong to think that his joy was postponed to the resurrection day. As he bent his will to the agony of the cross and the confrontation with Sin, we can believe that there was joy in the realisation that he was defeating iniquity and redeeming men from death and corruption. He was able to despise the shame because in the moment of its worst assault he had a consciousness of the final and ultimate joy of salvation. In the great prayer recorded in John 17, Jesus said to his Father about the disciples: "These things I speak in the world, that they may have my joy fulfilled in themselves" (v. 13). That prayer was answered at Philippi. Men, who through joy sing in prison, cannot really be imprisoned.

A Fruit of the Spirit

The foregoing should convince us that joy is not one great moment of ecstasy which comes in a crisis, lasts for a day, and then is gone. The point we are stressing is that joy is not circumstantial, but is independent of circumstances. One proof of this is in Galatians 5:22. Paul says: "The fruit of the spirit is love, joy, peace . . . " It does not matter whether you believe that the qualities listed are different fruits or that there is one fruit, love, and all that follow are the flavours, colours, textures of the one fruit.

Whichever way you look at it, joy is part of the fruit of the spirit. Fruit is not a flash-in-the-pan thing. It is permanent, solid, substantial. The growth is real but often imperceptible. Slowness is not failure. It is there on dull days as well as sunshine days. If joy sings it never tires. There is a song for June and a song for January. The word for joy is a common word. It is not a red-letter word, flaming with passion. It means something steady, quiet, divinely wonderful, like fruit. It means gladness, common delight—a sense of quiet assurance.

Those men at Philippi knew beyond any doubt that they were not alone. They knew in their deepest hearts that all things were working together for good under the providential hand of God. Bodily they seemed to be in the hand of the jailer, but spiritually they knew they were in the hand of God. As it turned out even the jailer was part of the great purpose: very soon he is washing their stripes. They had an unalterable conviction that nothing could separate them from the love of Christ. They trusted in the profound secret that the city was being built and that one day it would come down out of heaven from God. They knew that no power on earth could prevent it, and they were part of it. Sin was defeated; pardon was full and free; death was vanquished. The King was alive for evermore. This gives cause for joy and joy gives cause for song.

Delight from doing God's Will

Another cause for joy is obedience. Remember the words inscribed about the Redeemer: "I delight to do thy will, O my God" (Psalm 40:8). Delight is joy and joy comes from doing God's will. Ask any man who is flirting with sin, who plays the fool with his discipleship, and he will tell you that in the deepest part of him there is no joy. Conscience gives him no peace; neglect spoils his tranquillity. For the moment he may enjoy the satisfaction of the flesh, but afterwards the remorse brings only misery. There is no joy in disobedience.

One proof is in the life of the king Saul. Is there a sadder picture in the whole of the Bible than Saul creeping through the darkness of the night, seeking a witch woman in violation of his own edict? A king, who once was chosen by God, entering the black market of evil. The whole picture is full of fear and foreboding, and one thing there is not—there is no joy. Joy comes from obedience. Jesus said: "Blessed are they who hear the word of God and keep it." That blessedness is rich with joy. Some object to this point of view on the grounds that it will make us self-satisfied and wrongly superior. They are confusing joy with smugness. That believers can get smug there is no doubt, but it is not likely to come through faithful obedience to God's word and will. It is more likely to come by feverish activity trying to make up for the lack of true spiritual submission.

Finally, think of the impediments to joy. Doubt is one—that spirit which is always without complete conviction; always worrying over problems; nursing a voice inside which every day intrudes on the side of scepticism. Jude says we must be very merciful to those who find faith hard and doubt easy. Joy is difficult for them. Another hindrance is fear. Very often it is fear of the judgement seat: not that reverential fear which is an essential part of worship and service, but that fear which tends towards dread. Those with this burden so often see the eyes of fire and rarely hear the voice of love. The judgement is a solemn thing but it is not intended to rob us of joy. God is not an ogre who is trying to trap us into perdition. He is a loving Father who has gone to the uttermost to save us for Himself. He wants us to succeed. For those who seek joy, let them cast their burden on the Lord. "He will never leave thee nor forsake thee."

17

LOVE

"A NEW COMMANDMENT I GIVE UNTO YOU"

IF READING books about love could make us loving, then the quest would be over and the problem would be solved. In the religious world, it is probable that love has been written about more than any other subject. It shows how important love is. It is to discipleship what air is to respiration. One without the other has no reality. This is the argument of the Apostle Paul in 1 Corinthians 13. He lists all the eminent expressions of discipleship—speaking the truth with inspired voices; understanding the deep things of God with spiritual insight; having faith so as to act boldly in the cause of Christ; being instant upon pastoral care; making yourself poor for the poor's sake; ready to sacrifice all, even life itself, for the Gospel.

He lists them all with eloquent sentences and then says that without love they are nothing. These good works may well help others as they are done. In the execution there may well be benefit for the other party. Objectively they may well be valuable. But for the disciple who does them without love, his discipleship is helped not one whit. Like a sounding brass and a tinkling symbal—a sound without significance. If the judgement seems hard, remember it is the judgement of an inspired apostle. To disciples surrounded with all kinds of gifts and graces, his solemn advice is this—follow after love. That is the best spiritual ambition.

First of all let us hear the testimony of Jesus in John 13:34-35: "A new commandment I give unto you, that ye love one another; even as I have loved you, that ye also love one another. By this shall all men know that ye are my disciples, if ye have love one to

77

another.'' Notwithstanding all the other important marks of discipleship, according to Jesus this exercise of love is the supreme distinction. This is the incisive test.

Next the testimony of John in 1 John 2:7-8: ''Beloved, no new commandment write I unto you, but an old commandment which ye had from the beginning: the old commandment is the word which ye heard. Again, a new commandment write I unto you, which thing is true in him and in you; because the darkness is passing away, and the true light already shineth.'' Notice John does not say precisely what the new commandment is. He goes on, of course, that if you hate your brother you are in darkness and if you love your brother you are in the light—so you may well deduce what the new commandment is about.

But speculation is not really necessary because to join the words of Jesus to the words of John is to know surely that the new commandment in both cases is the commandment to love one another. Return to the First Epistle of John and mark John's exposition of its history. The first thing he says about the new commandment is that it is old. He says he is telling something which has been heard from the beginning. By the beginning he cannot mean the beginning of the Gospel, because in the Gospel of John the commandment is called new. Its oldness was this: the words which call Israel to love are there on the parchment of Deuteronomy 6 and Leviticus 19 and are well known to all disciples. So he was right, this Hebrew fisherman—it was an old commandment and it was there right at the beginning of the nationhood of Israel.

The Newness of the Old Commandment

Yet here is the problem: Jesus calls it new and so does John sequentially. Why is this and wherein is its novelty to be discovered? First of all, as revealed by the Lord and as confirmed by John, it was new in its extent. The difference between the old and the new would be discovered in an understanding about to whom the love was to be applied: put another way, how the words ''one another'' were to be measured. To the Hebrews it meant only other Hebrews—they had no truck with the Gentiles. Then it was narrowed further to mean Hebrews who are your friends. By the time Jesus came to announce the new commandment, the old one had come to mean, as he said, ''Thou shalt love thy neighbour and hate thine enemy". Now the new commandment said an outrageous thing: "Love your enemies."

It flung back the frontiers and broke through the barriers. Not just those whom you like and who like you: there was nought new in that—it had been going on for two millennia. No: to the word "neighbour" Jesus, with sweet satire, gave a new interpretation. As an example of a neighbour he chose somebody the Jews had come to despise—a Samaritan. Love him, said Jesus. This was new; a call to love which broke through the entrenched positions of the rabbis and the lawyers. The imperial voice of the Messiah was seeking to provoke the narrowest and most insular people in the world to a spirit of universal compassion. And those who responded were in the truest sense to become peculiar people. The world would know them as these strange people who love one another without distinction and without partiality. The followers of the Man of Nazareth, the virgin-born, the ever-living. This then was the first measurement of its newness—its extent.

Love as a Principle

The next definition of its newness would be its principle. Up to the time that the Messiah spoke to his people, obedience had been demanded and regulated by law. You break the law and you suffer the penalty—therefore if you are sensible you do not break the law. Perhaps you would like to break the law, but because you are afraid of the consequences, you are law-abiding.

Suffer an illustration. Imagine one disciple is sorely provoked by another. Inwardly passions rage. But in the provocation the injured brother does his comrade no harm. Why is this? What controls his restraint? Is it that he knows that if he retaliated they would lock him up for a long time? Is it a case of "I would, but I dare not"? No: it is because their relationship is love-mastered. He does not need the law to stop him being a murderer or injurious, because under the compulsion of love a man is free from fear of the law.

Ponder this: why are you obedient? Is it dread of discovery if you are not, or is it something higher? If you are love-mastered then the law is, in a sense, superfluous. So one day a man is going to write: "Love is the fulfilling of the law." Recall this from 1 Timothy 1:9: "Knowing this, that the law is not made for a righteous man, but for the lawless and disobedient, for the ungodly and for sinners, for the unholy and the profane, for murderers of fathers and murderers of mothers, for manslayers, for whoremongers . . . '' The principle is this: rise into the spirit of love and you are free from the restraints of the law. So it is not a case of, ''I would, but I dare not''. It is a case of, ''I could, but I will not—for love's sake''. In other words, because of the law of love which drives you, you cannot harm your brother, you cannot degrade one of your Father's other children. The new man, the new-born, love-dominated spirit will do no evil to his fellow men. It transcends law and rests upon this blessed principle of love. It was the proclamation of this in the simple reality of life which was new.

Love is Sacrificial

Then finally, but pre-eminently, it was new in its intensity. Return to 1 John 2:8, and notice the words precisely: ''Again, a new commandment I write unto you, which thing is true in him and in you; because the darkness is past, and the true light now shineth.'' It seems that John is saying that the realisation of the new commandment is truly revealed in Jesus our Lord: ''which thing is true in him''—he has manifested its meaning.

When you go back to the Gospel the method of the manifestation is revealed: ''A new commandment I give unto you, that ye love one another *as I have loved you*.'' There is the measurement and there is the revelation—''As I have loved you''. John said, ''Which thing is true in him''. If you would know and understand the real nature of the new commandment, then mark his love-impulsed life.

Understand this: Christ's love was not superficial; it was sacrificial. ''Greater love hath no man than this, that a man lay down his life for his friends.'' Without dispute this is what he did. Even his enemies testified that this was true. They said, taunting him in the hour of his agony: ''He saved others, himself he cannot save.'' In their anxiety to condemn him they admitted that he had saved others. Further, in order to do it, he would not save himself. So when he said, ''as I have loved you'', it cost him his life to give the declaration its true meaning. It teaches us that love measured by Christ's example is sacrificial.

Therefore the new commandment, interpreted by his life, is saying to us a very challenging thing. Love—though it may cost you dear. Love—though it may never be repaid. Love—though men rend your heart. Love—and keep your spirit from being hardened and embittered. The love of Jesus was a trusting love. Although his disciples were weak and afraid and unworthy, he clung tenaciously to the belief that in the end they would respond and be all he intended—and so they were. This reveals the intensity of the new commandment: it is sacrificial. This revelation was new.

"Love never faileth"

Finally, think of this. Love and hate have one thing in common —they both increase at compound interest. If you try doing good to someone, ere long, you will come to regard them differently. The spirit of love will ennoble your relationship. Act lovingly and you will come to love, even the most unlikely people. The unloved, the forgotten, the introverted—those whom Jesus called *the least* of these his brethren.

Here is a solemn thought. How you love the least may at last decide your final reward. Love and hate are cumulative in their effect. Every act of hatred makes you more harsh, more suspicious, more selfish. Every act of love makes you more compassionate, more selfless, more loving: in the sight of God, more lovely. Just as one act of submission to the Father makes you more a son or daughter, so one act of love makes you more like Christ.

The important thing to remember is that what we believe about love has in the end to be made incarnate, if love is to be real. It is no good having warm thoughts and cold spirits. Love, in the final reality, is a practical thing. We shall develop this in the next chapter.

18

LOVE
"THE FRUIT OF THE SPIRIT"

BY common consent the finest and best analysis of love in the Bible is in 1 Corinthians 13. Why it was revealed first to the believers at Corinth we cannot tell—perhaps they needed it most. But for all disciples it is a masterpiece. Love divided so as to make love complete; an apocalypse of spiritual life lived in the standing ground of human need and human weakness. Love on the earth battling against the things which are unlovely. Love positively active, for goodness sake; a blueprint of how the theory works. Love leavens life. Every virtue is impregnated. No part of discipleship escapes the influence of love.

The plan now is to examine the sentences in 1 Corinthians 13 and to seek to identify the ways of love by single words common to the life of faith, a reduction of the analysis to the everyday forces of discipleship.

1 Corinthians 13

Verse 4	"Love suffereth long . . . "	*Longsuffering*
	" . . . and is kind"	*Kindness*
	" . . . envieth not; vaunteth not itself, is not puffed up"	*Meekness*
Verse 5	"Doth not behave itself unseemly": that is, behaviour out of control. The Bible word for self-control is:	*Temperance*

82

	" . . . taketh not account of evil": positively, that is "taketh account of good"	*Goodness*
Verse 6	"Rejoiceth not in iniquity, but rejoiceth in the truth"	*Joy*
Verse 7	"Beareth all things, believeth all things, hopeth all things, endureth all things": a sense of tranquillity, of undisturbedness. Put it with the "not easily provoked" of verse 5 and you have peacefulness of soul.	*Peace*
Verse 8	"Love never faileth". That which never fails is constant. The Bible word for constancy is:	*Faithfulness*

Put the list together: longsuffering, kindness, meekness, temperance, goodness, joy, peace, faithfulness. Familiar words? Re-arrange them and they become even more familiar, like this: joy, peace, longsuffering, kindness, goodness, faithfulness, meekness, temperance. As we read the words their place is remembered: Galatians 5:22, the fruit of the spirit. Previously we have hinted that there are people who believe that there is only one fruit of the spirit, that is love, and all the words which follow in Galatians 5:22 are the colours, textures and flavours of the one fruit. It means that all these blessed virtues are in one way or another an expression of love in action: love, the fruit of the spirit in all its varied forms; loveliness multiplied in loving diversity. Let us examine it carefully and discover the force of love in the fruit of the spirit.

Joy: Once before we stressed that joy is not one blinding flash of ecstatic happiness which comes suddenly and then is gone. It is a constant force of common delight which is undisturbed by circumstances, good or bad; in a sense detached from the undulations of life but always sensitive to the needs they create. That means that joy cannot be enjoyed in isolation. Joy cannot be hoarded. When joy is gathered it is gathered in order to be spread. It is not drinking at the stream to quench our thirst alone: it is drinking for the common wealth; it is taking the water into the desert for thirsty souls; it is putting a little sweetness into the drabness of somebody's day, a little companionship into somebody's loneliness. Joy active is moved by the impetus of love for some other soul.

Peace: We have referred before to the peace of the tranquil pond covered with weed. But that peace of stagnation is not the peace which is love mastered. True Biblical peace is the harmony of opposing forces, concord where otherwise there might be strife. It is not the burying of the hatchet for the sake of quietness. Hatchets can be dug up and too often they are. Peace through love means ending strife and bringing harmony because of love for those who are estranged, making peace for love of him who said, "Blessed are the peacemakers". Peace is the ministry of healing. It is not always easy, but let us know that at its head there is a file leader and he is called "the Prince of Peace".

Longsuffering: It is an old-fashioned word. A more modern equivalent might be "long-temperedness". It is having infinite patience. Some people say, "I am quick tempered; I cannot help it". The writer has sympathy, but knows we must *try* to help it. It calls us to resist the temptation, so often faced, when we say, "I have put up with this long enough . . .". The only force which will make short-tempered people into long-sufferers is love. How often have we heard it! We say, "Why she puts up with it I cannot tell . . . " The explanation may be that she is long-suffering. Do not be too harsh with her. Remember, "Love suffers long and then speaks its mind"? That must be a different Bible. Remember rather, "Love suffereth long *and is kind*". Hear it again: "Love beareth all things, believeth all things, hopeth all things, endureth all things": not *some* things, but *all* things. This is long-temperedness.

Kindness: Vine's *Dictionary* says that this word has the idea of goodness of heart with an especial reference to service. It is more than having kind thoughts—it is a very practical word. James would have liked it. He knew that blankets are better than talk. It is not doing great things occasionally; it is doing small things regularly, and not minding that they seem so small. It is having a keen-eyed but unobtrusive capacity to discern the need and to meet it lovingly. Fame and reward have no place here. Put simply, kindness is love communicating.

Goodness: The writer remembers reading once that children are good, adults are righteous. That may be, but by this word adults are called to be good as well. It is a divine word. God said to Moses, "I will let all my goodness pass before thee" and it revealed the glory of the Lord. It means doing good things and refusing to do bad things. Joseph is a good example: "How can I do this great evil and sin against God?" It is love of that which is good and hatred of that which is evil; doing good for the love of God and for the love of those who love you; refusing evil because it may break somebody's heart.

Goodness in order to be respectable is one thing—goodness for love's sake is another. David once came to Jerusalem and said: "Are there any here of the house of Saul whom I may love for Jonathan's sake?" And they brought to him poor Mephibosheth, who was lame in both feet and lived in obscurity. David set him at the royal table and cared for him. That is goodness: doing good for love's sake.

Faithfulness: This has to do with integrity. It is another word for fidelity. It means being faithful to your word: true to your accepted responsibility, whether in business, in marriage, in the ecclesia. It outlaws the thought of shirking or shedding your duty, be the reason ever so plausible. It means being very careful about your promises and about your relationship with others. It means being ready to give up your own special preferences, your own scruples, your own strong opinions, if they may hinder your brother or sister or cause them to sin. It means loyalty to the Truth, even if it means a diminution of your rights, an interference with your progress, risking your reputation. It will garrison a disciple against the possibility of filling his mouth with other people's faults when he ought to ponder his own. How on earth will people behave faithfully in the face of these temptations?—only through love, love of God, love of the truth, love of God's other children.

Meekness: A speaker once said that to be meek you have to be unconscious. He was probably right. Conscious humility tends to be contrived. But it is not easy. Some virtues can be practised, but not meekness. As the man said, it is unconscious. Doing good sometimes makes people puffed up. The best advice seems to be to do your work for Christ faithfully and try not to think about yourself. Do not look for opportunities to do great things—you may have to wait half a lifetime. Do the commonplace well and faithfully. Do not mind that it seems so commonplace. There is nothing menial in the service of the King. The New Testament writers proceed in the belief that the driving force for our labour of love is the love of the Redeemer—understood and realised. They say, "The love of Christ constraineth us". If we really believe it we are not so likely to get puffed up. We may even become meek.

Temperance: This describes, or has come to describe, a special kind of abstinence: abstinence from intoxicating liquor. The problem is that the absolute nature of teetotalism may in a way be intemperate. Be that as it may, the real meaning of temperance in this passage is *self-control*. This is a hard thing to achieve if you are prompted by the wrong motives. Control through fear is a struggle which is likely to end in failure. Control for the sake of respectability or through anxiety to avoid detection is at best fragile. Sometimes if the circumstances change, the control is abandoned. When all is said and done the best motive for self-control is love. If we take care of our behaviour—that is, we exercise the use of our freedom carefully, in consideration of our brethren and sisters, that is the highest motive of all and most likely to succeed. Love of our brethren: love desiring their advancement; love seeking their salvation—what a blessing it is so to live your life that none of God's family is ever harmed but rather blessed and encouraged, strengthened and provoked to love and good works. Disciples moved by temperance have shed their hobnail boots. They walk gently and circumspectly for love's sake. Temperance is the triumph of love.

The fruit of the Spirit is love—and if you can receive it, these are the flavours, textures, colours: different and detectable but all part of the one fruit. Remember one thing: fruit is not magic. It does not appear overnight: growth is real but slow. Protection and cultivation are vital. Setbacks there will be. Waiting and working are not always contradictory. Let us never lose heart. It is, after all, the fruit of the Spirit. Fruit is God-created, not man-made.

19

PRINCIPLES OF PROGRESS

"THIS ONE THING I DO . . . "

IT GOES almost without saying that progress is an integral part of the genius of discipleship. There is movement on the narrow road and, be it ever so slow, it ought to be movement forward. After all, those who are newborn must grow and if they do not we call it arrested development. Every disciple, therefore, ought to be concerned about making spiritual progress. Sometimes the progress is imperceptible but that is not failure. Magic is one thing; steady progress in the tide of spiritual living is another. Every sorrow, every joy, every deepening understanding of God's purpose, every experience of temptation faced and mastered should be a stepping stone to a stronger foothold.

It has to be admitted that this is not always the case. Sometimes, especially when the temptation is not mastered, the faculties seem paralysed and the will is fettered. But to fall is not to surrender. If soldiers abandoned the fight because sometimes they were halted, no battle would ever be won. From the new position they take stock and plan the next advance. Sometimes forward, sometimes backward, but as the sun westers they are forward from where it dawned, be the advance ever so small. So it is with the life of discipleship. That being accepted, this chapter is concerned with some of the principles which regulate progress, and the first to be considered can be described in three words: *forget the past*.

The first likely reaction is that it needs qualification, and it does. More than once the Bible urges us to *remember* the past. As the people of God faced the untrodden pathway Moses said: "Ye shall remember all the way that the Lord thy God hath led thee." Remembrance of the past can be very beneficial, because sometimes it generates hope for the future. The providence of the past can become providence for the future. Faced with a flooded river you can remember crossing the Red Sea. He who led once can lead again. In Psalm 42 David describes how his soul was cast down. In the midst of his distress he falls back on his memory of what God has done. He says: "I remember Hermon and Jordan and Mizar." So his faith was sustained by remembrance of the past.

All this is true, but in the third chapter of the Philippian letter, on the very subject of making progress, the apostle Paul says categorically: *"This one thing I do"*—meaning, leaving all other things and concentrating on the one thing that matters—"Forgetting the things which are behind, I press forward . . . " (v. 13). Let us detain ourselves just for a moment to take encouragement from this picture of the great apostle: a man striving and struggling to make progress. It tells us that what we feel, he felt also. Seeking, reaching onward, sometimes hindered but always hopeful, he pressed forward toward the mark. The message is that what was true for Paul is true for us, and his first great piece of advice is this: forget the past.

Faith through Fire

Let us not get it out of perspective. Forgetting the past is not everything, but it has a part. The part it may occupy in individual lives will vary according to circumstances. It may not be your particular problem but it may be somebody's somewhere. Think of this situation. There are some people who look back and long for the days of innocence; that is, the days when we knew nothing really of evil. There are those who think that the innocent days were the holiest and the purest—but it is an illusion.

Real goodness has to be fought out in the face of those forces which, apart from God, would doom us. Soldiers are not proved in the military college but on the field of battle. Faith is made stronger as it passes through the fire. Sometimes children are shielded from the world excessively—every adversity or trial is kept from them; every book, paper and companion censored. At last they have to face the world, innocent in the wrong way: ill equipped to face the real world because the hot-house of the kindergarten has been falsely prolonged, the evil day only delayed; and the awful experience when it comes is worse than it need be because of the ignorance of the man who was still really a child. So forget the age of innocence. It was worth something at the right time, but now it is worth little. "When I was a child, I thought as a child . . . but now I am a man I put away childish things."

Then think of this: the past is irreparable. Brooding on it cannot change it. That truth may be the agony of our life but it is unassailable. Detain ourselves again to say that if we have recently done something hard or foolish, let us put it right without delay, else it may haunt us all our days. If we have slammed the door hard, let us heal the breach quickly. It is a terrible thing to have said our last word to someone we ought to love and to have said it bitterly. It may really be the last word.

Remorse—or Resolution?

Remember the past is irreparable. Sometimes people look back and brood upon the past disappointedly: so much hoped for, so little achieved; the time squandered, the opportunities missed. We were hindered by our own indolence or our own wilfulness. But it is done now. We cannot alter the past. Remorse can be a curse if it inhibits the will to strive on hopefully and manfully. The past is an obstacle if it robs us of resolution for today and tomorrow.

The best way to look at the past is to enquire if the things which are behind are in some sense in front. This may seem topsy-turvy but words do not always mean what they seem to mean. The writer recalls a story told some time ago by an old friend about a man who was always late for the board meetings of his company. The chairman wrote to him complaining, and the man replied like this: "I admit that before I have been behind, but in future all that will be in the past. I think you will agree that I have been early of late."

So the question to ask is this: are the things which are behind still in front of you?—the things which you detached from your life in the first full flush of discipleship. The things about which at first you were very strict—are they still with you? Have they in some sense been reinstated? Has your strictness given way to tolerance? The things which at one time you were glad to lose, counting them well lost—have they been retrieved secretly? The bridges you burned at first—have you crept back quietly and rebuilt them? Not bad things, not evil things—but things which hinder and halt: neutral in themselves, but in the context of discipleship—*weights*. Old habits, old status, old friends, old prestige, old things in which you once trusted. We must face these things because Paul said, "Forgetting the things which are behind . . . " So there is the situation that the past cannot be forgotten while we keep it and nurse it.

We have to be fair—there are some things which can never be erased from the memory. You cannot *will* to forget. Try forgetting to think of giraffes. No—it does not work, but you can will not to think of things mournfully and morbidly in such a way as to produce a rueful, self-accusing temper which has the effect of hindering progress in real godliness. To dwell in a melancholic spirit upon past mistakes is like indulging again in the very thing which ought to be repudiated and forgotten. There are some people who traverse again and again the path of sin and in that journey secretly find some satisfaction: a fantasy relived and enjoyed. Making light of sin is an awful thing, but perhaps brooding over it is as bad.

Look Forward! Press Forward!

If a man in good faith strives to forget past sin he is doing what the God of forgiveness wants him to do. For if God forgets the sin which is pardoned, why should the sinner revive it through remorse? Remember it was wrongful remorse which fixed Judas in his awful destiny. Sometimes remorse paralyses present endeavour. Yes, we are guilty; we have pleaded for pardon; we have sought to make amends; we have learned the lesson. Let us leave it there with God. Forget the sinful past. Keep a broad back to the years that the locusts have eaten. Keep a full face to the appointed goal.

Finally this: remember that looking back sadly is the particular business of the man or woman without hope. They cannot look forward for there is nothing to look forward to. There is no spring for the godless be they ever so brash. *Your* high calling is to look forward and to press forward. Let God deal with the past. You can be sure He has and He will. It may be that out of the past there is some chastisement for our salvation, but if there is, God will deal with it for our good and never for our harming, as He did with Jacob. If there is something in your past which haunts you, which nothing in these sentences can help or change—then let God come between you and your past. The promise of the Truth in Christ Jesus is that in him there is rest for the wearied soul and healing for the wounded spirit. Into one place are gathered all the failure, all the sin and all the shame—and there by one act of atonement are they cancelled and forgotten. Let us leave the past, because the past forgotten is strength realised and progress made.

It is true that forgetting the past is largely a negative thing. In the next chapter we shall look at something more positive in the cause of progress—mastering the hindrances.

20

PRINCIPLES OF PROGRESS

"LET US LAY ASIDE EVERY WEIGHT"

L OOK again and carefully at the words of the Apostle Paul
about making progress: "Brethren, I count not myself to have
apprehended: but this one thing I do, forgetting those things which
are behind, and reaching forth unto those things which are before,
I press toward the mark for the prize of the high calling of God in
Christ Jesus" (Phil. 3:13,14). In the last chapter we considered the
matter of forgetting the things which are behind. We have now to
ponder the business of reaching forward and pressing onward.
Paradoxically, as a step in that direction, leave the figure of
running the race and come to another, the growth of the seed.

Given the right conditions, growth is a divinely natural thing.
You cannot make things grow by resolution or affirmation. Jesus
said: "Which of you by taking thought can add one cubit unto his
stature?" Establish the conditions of growth and growth will
occur: not by magic but by a wonderful process of enlargement by
development from within. Now here is a thing to understand: one
of the vital conditions to establish in order to advance growth is
removal of the hindrances.

Master the Hindrances

Think of your own garden: when it is free of pests and weeds
and diseases, given the right feeding, growth flourishes. When
growth diminishes and plants become weary and withered, it is
nearly always due to some horticultural hindrance—beetles, blight
and bindweed. The teaching of Jesus confirms it. In the parable
of the sower the unfruitful seed was unfruitful because of some

hindrance to growth—rocky subsoil, weeds, hungry birds. The fruitful seed flourished in good soil free from hindrances. So here emerges an important principle of progress—*master the hindrances*.

If you return to the figure with which we began, the running of the race, the principle is still true: "Let us lay aside every weight, and the sin which doth so easily beset us, and let us run with patience the race that is set before us" (Heb. 12:1). Weights are hindrances and the teaching of the writer to the Hebrews is that they have to be mastered in the cause of victory. How often has the runner said that he made a good start and was in a good position, *but*—then follows the something which hindered him from pressing forward and onward to breast the tape. Nobody in their right mind would run in hobnail boots and an overcoat, but some hindrances are far less obvious and more subtle. Whatever they are, for progress to be made they have to be mastered. Once long ago the ecclesias in Galatia were faltering and the apostle Paul diagnosed their trouble like this: "Ye did run well: who did hinder you that ye should not obey the truth?"

Measure the Problem

Recollect again Hebrews 12:1: "Let us lay aside every weight . . ." What are weights? Strangely enough a weight is not a burden. A burden is some adversity which we have to bear and cannot shed—for our own sake or someone else's. A weight is some hindrance which impedes our spiritual progress which we could shed if we like, but which for some reason or another we do not. It would not be right to think that weights are always some form of adversity. Indeed there are some kinds of adversity which in the long run have proved to be blessings, because they have a chastening effect upon the soul.

Sometimes weights could never be recognised as adversity because they are so nice. Chastening is sent by God but God does not send weights. God does not hinder people who want to progress in their pilgrimage to His kingdom. A weight is a hindrance—an impediment. It slows down the progress, it puts the brakes on, it makes the road go uphill when it need not. Weights are bad if you mean business about making progress. An unnecessary encumbrance, best cast off but often retained because we want the best of both worlds.

An honest examination of a disciple's life would unmask the things which ought to be known for what they are and the weights would come out of hiding ready to be recognised and repudiated. Sometimes our hindrances are self-made—an indulgence which gives us particular pleasure but which has the effect of lowering the standard; some association which robs us of enthusiasm for the Truth; some enterprise which would make us ashamed if the truth were known. These forces are self-chosen and we cannot blame others or other things for our own wilfulness. On the other hand some hindrances are almost wholly circumstantial. Some disciples' work: they were pushed into it when they were young and they have never been able to escape. A disciple's marriage: it started right but deteriorated. A disciple's education: it was of the wrong kind and developed tendencies which hinder and drag down in the search for the right way.

Sometimes hindrances are in themselves good things but because they are wrongly used become weights. Invested with too much power or conceded too much authority they hold back and distract. Money is not evil. Pleasure is not wrong. Business is not sinful. Friendship is not harmful. Education is no snare. Yet all these are reasons why sometimes people fail and falter on the road to the kingdom. Sometimes the good is the enemy of the best. When the man found the pearl of great price he had to sell his other *good* pearls to get the best. In a way the good almost becomes evil when it keeps us from something better. Indeed it may be one thing only. It seems unfair: a good life hindered by one thing. The trouble is that very often it is the one thing that matters. We have been over this territory already in this book but no harm will be done to recollect that sometimes a fair prospect can be blighted by one unmastered hindrance.

Administer the Sentence

The question is: How are hindrances to be dealt with? One thing is certain: procrastination can be a snare. Remember Paul's words to the Galatians: "Who doth hinder you, *that ye should not obey the truth*?" Hindrances unmastered and fostered can lead to a worse condition. But plainly—doing nothing is doing the worst. Paul says there is one thing to do: after forgetting the past, press on to the future. Stretch forward. In other words, let nothing hold you back. With that determination, the hindrances have to give way.

Put simply, it is necessary to take firm action. Tinkering ends in torsion. Flirting leads to frustration. There is nothing like a clean break. At all costs avoid the temptation. Go home the long way if that is necessary. Say no, not any more. Give up the indulgence. End the association. Abandon the enterprise. "This one thing I do." Well, do it. Get on your knees and pray, then get on your feet and act. Sometimes men are on their knees when they should be on their feet, but true disciples know that trusting and trying are not contradictory: they are complementary.

Act Immediately

It has to be admitted that circumstantial hindrances are more difficult. It sometimes appears that nothing can be done—what cannot be cured has to be endured. But there are disciples who would testify that when all seemed hopeless, hope was renewed. When the future was blank, a door was opened. When the soul was cast down, relief came, and the hindrance was shed. Even when circumstances seem unalterable, it is a good thing never to accept inevitability. Seem to take some action, however improbable it may appear.

Think of Zacchaeus in Luke 19. He was a man beset with hindrances. He was in a bad profession where sin was easy. He had a bad reputation, so there was nothing to live up to. He was rich. Then in addition he was short of stature. On the day the king came to Jericho that was a particular hindrance. He wanted to see the Rabbi and could not. Some people might have advised Zacchaeus to give up his desire and consult a specialist with a view to taking a course for making short people tall. But Zacchaeus's need was urgent. Perhaps he had heard that this man of Nazareth was able to shed peace upon restless spirits, to give new hope to rejected people. He had to take action there and then.

Poor Zacchaeus was in earnest—you have to be when you are mastered by hindrances. This one thing he did—he climbed a tree. It was an act of faith. Let us not mistake it—that was Zacchaeus's part in the path of progress. Notice God's part. "Zacchaeus, make haste, and come down, for I must abide at thy house." In making spiritual progress there is man's part and there is God's part. God, because He is our Father, will never fail us. But just as God's part is vital, so is man's. Dilly-dallying is deadly. Do what has to be done, in faith. Probably more people miss the highest and descend to the lowest through the matter of postponement of the one thing that ought to be done, than through any other cause. One little phrase in the story of Zacchaeus is so telling: "therefore he ran . . .". When the long record of discipleship comes to be unveiled and those are noticed who have made progress on the way to life, it could well show that at the crucial time, when the tide was at the flood, they *ran* and did what had to be done. Casting aside their procrastination, they pressed forward. Laying aside their weights, they ran the race.

The man who first said, "Let us lay aside every weight", also said, "Today if ye will hear his voice, harden not your hearts." Remember this—it is not only a word of warning, it is also the good news of immediate possibility. If you hear his voice and obey, progress will come.

21

WORSHIP

"A RIGHT SPIRIT"

HOW easy it is, even in one sentence, to make a mistake. When the opening sentences of this chapter were being planned they were going to set forth the idea that worship is realised on two levels, the external and the spiritual. So it would have been inferred that if something is external it is not spiritual. That would have been a mistake. The external forms of worship are important and valid *and* spiritual, but only if they are counterparts of that inner spirit of worship, which we shall come to ere long.

When disciples are reverent externally it ought to be because they are first reverent internally. When disciples bow their heads in visible worship, it ought to be because they have first submitted themselves to God in the quiet recesses of their life. External worship is spiritual when it is the outcome of an internal spiritual condition. One is the outcome of the other. But we have to recognise that the process works the other way round. That is to say: sometimes the external form of worship will induce in those who participate a reverent spirit. Sometimes the very nature of the assembly will provoke in the hearts of those who have come, a worshipful attitude. How often has it happened that we have come with our spirits disturbed and our hearts wrongly impulsed and we have gone away calmed and satisfied? have bowed our heads in reverent and filial fear, confessed our need and thanked God and worshipped Him in spirit and in truth? It happened because the spirit of the assembly touched us, and brought us rest and healing.

Notice then how important it must be to strive for the very highest quality in our corporate and external acts of worship. It may be a humbling thing to have to confess but it is true, that external things can affect our inward spirit so much. Sometimes we are at the mercy of infinitesimals. Trivial things disturb us. What seems to help one hinders another. Certain forms of music evoke worshipful feelings in one and retard them in another.

Obviously this is a matter which is highly subjective. We all have our favourite hymns and sometimes we think they must be approved in heaven because they suit us so well. To some extent it may be that our preferences are conditioned by our upbringing. Once more, the child is father to the man. What we were taught to like when we were young, remains with us still. We must therefore be patient with other people's choices. We must be tolerant with those who have not had the advantage of being reared in the atmosphere of the Truth.

Religious Experience and External Forms

Feelings about worship, in its external expression, vary according to one's early religious experience. For example, we do not regard our meeting rooms as temples because we remember that God is not worshipped any longer in temples made with hands. But some disciples cannot escape the feeling that where God is worshipped must in some sense be a holy place. They like to feel the atmosphere of reverence. They think that if the spirit is to be hushed, quietness will help. It is perfectly true that God can be worshipped in the market place, but it is a different style of worship from the sanctuary. There the worshippers, coming to show their reverence in the presence of the most high God, expect that the market place will be excluded. So we have to be tolerant of other people's feelings about reverence. We cannot lay down the law about details because there is no law. All things are to be done decently and in order and this we strive for. From time to time today we pass resolutions calling for greater reverence. We say: less talking, more quiet. It is nothing new. In the writer's meeting they were doing it in 1910.

Unfairly, perhaps, the writer dares to take advantage of his readers and tell them of his own preferences. He wishes that in our services we sang the psalms as a regular feature. Not just paraphrases, but the psalms as they stand upon the parchment of the Old Testament. He wishes that somebody would put the words to the right kind of music and let us learn it—and then sing the psalms to the glory of God. But he is willing to admit that this desire might be something to do with his upbringing.

Some commentators stress that the essential meaning of the idea of worship in the Bible is that of prostration. The fundamental thought is that of bowing low and walking out backwards; a humble recognition of the absolute supremacy of God. It is doing obeisance in the presence of the throne. The idea compels men to an attitude of reverence in the realisation of the total superiority of God: an attitude which recognises that God is all sufficient for the needs of man; that man, apart from God, is altogether incomplete—unfulfilled and wasted; that all man needs is to be found in the resource and bounty of the great God of heaven; that men depend upon God. Man is the subject, God is the King.

This realisation produces the attitude of worship. It is this consciousness which makes the external form of worship spiritual. In the truest sense, by this means the song becomes sacred. The prayer is, in the truest sense, the raising of the heart and mind to heaven. Because of their consciousness of worship, the worshippers can cast their burdens upon the Lord. They trust in his power to meet every need. Their attention to the word of God, because of the spirit of worship, is reverent, eager and submissive. This corporate act of reverence is a holy thing. God says He will be sanctified in them that draw nigh before Him. Notwithstanding, it could be meaningless, without the spirit of worship born in the heart and provoking the mind to a condition of reverent fear. Without this the song will not penetrate the roof. We must know that it is possible to sing a humble song and inwardly to be as proud as a peacock. So with what awe should we draw near to worship! and we ought to be full of awe if we neglect it.

Motive is Vital

Think of Leviticus 10 and the two men who offered strange fire before the Lord. The rules of the old economy have faded but the principle remains. Motive always is the test of means. We may sing the song and pray the prayer but God looks on the heart. Those who draw nigh and stand in His presence must worship in spirit and in truth. In spirit—that is, it must not be external only, but must be matched by an inward spirit, submitted and reverent. In truth— that is, it must be based on a humble recognition of what God has revealed, not upon what man has invented. Those who come in spirit and in truth should be those who have enthroned God as their King and are ready to enquire with reverence about His will, so that it may become theirs. Two men, either carelessly or for convenience, ignored this, and the false fire became a consuming fire.

It does reveal that motive is vital, and it is this element that makes the worship true or false. It is a solemn thing to draw near in the place of reverent service and it ought to fill us with awe, but we have no right to say that because the responsibility is so solemn, therefore we will not come. That is the worst folly of all.

In the 19th chapter of the Apocalypse there is a vision of a great act of worship. The words are inspired and inspiring, a prophecy of praise. The great multitude cries "Hallelujah" and then there is a great responsive "Amen". Amen to His will and Praise to His name. In this case the praise was audible *and so was the Amen*. Could we not make this a pattern for our own worship? To say "Amen" with the voice and with the heart sets the seal upon true worship. The devotions are true worship if we have learned to say Amen in our lives and our living is a harmonious Hallelujah to God's praise.

In the light of the foregoing the writer has to confess to a worry. He wonders about the licence heaven grants concerning the difference between what we say and sing in our worship—and what we do in practice. It could be argued that we sing about aspirations and there is always a difference between aspiration and achievement. That is true, but sometimes the difference between what we sing and say and what we do is worrying. Think of this:

> "O may these heavenly pages be
> My ever dear delight;
> And still new beauties may I see
> And still increasing light."

If we sing that, true worship demands that we seek to make it true in our daily experience, pondering the word of God regularly. Or this:

> "O use me Lord, use even me
> Just as thou wilt, and when and where,
> Until thy blessed face I see,
> Thy rest, thy joy, thy glory share."

If we sing that, true worship demands that we strive to give the Truth's service top priority. This is the discipline of worship. Reverence compels us to mean what we say.

The writer judges no man; he is too conscious of his own failings to do that. He remembers though that more than once over the years he has prayed a prayer in one form or another that said to God that the world was a wicked place, full of corruption; that we are beset on every side and besieged; that we were in peril and without joy until the kingdom comes—and then afterwards went to a comfortable home in a commodious car, to serve in a profession, which judged by some standards was profitable, and managed to live quite happily in this wicked world and discover a fair bit of joy from it one way or another.

This teaches us, or should, that sincere worship is genuinely a kind of discipline and the very attempt to be sincere makes us strive to live more nearly in accordance with the things we sing and say in the holy place. On the other hand, it may teach us not to say extravagant things if we do not mean them. The important thing is never to devalue the spirit of worship by empty words and hollow ritual.

In the next chapter, we shall try to look more closely at worship in the daily life of discipleship.

22

WORSHIP

"TO THE GLORY OF GOD, THE FATHER"

THIS chapter is concerned with worship in the daily experience of discipleship. Let us seek to begin on the highest level by coming to rock bottom. Suppose the question is asked as to what is the real purpose of worship? A fair answer would be to praise, exalt and honour God. This definition provokes a further question, namely, how is it accomplished in the daily experience of discipleship? Think of Psalm 96:8,9: "Give unto the Lord the glory due unto his name . . . O worship the Lord in the beauty of holiness." Or Revelation 14:7: "Fear God, and give glory to him; for the hour of his judgment is come: and worship him that made heaven, and earth, and the sea, and the fountains of waters." In both these quotations there is an equivalence between giving glory to God and giving Him worship.

So to understand this aspect of worship we must follow the idea of giving glory to God. We shall find it is utterly fundamental. In Isaiah 43 the prophet says that man was made to give glory to God: "Every one that is called by my name, and whom I have created for my glory; I have formed him; yea, I have made him" (v. 7). It is true that the words were spoken in the first intention of the people of Israel, but remember that in a certain sense Israel are representative. God was showing in one nation what He would do for all nations at last. "In thee shall all families of the earth be blessed" was the promise to Abraham. The elect race of the Old Testament, essentially Hebrew, becomes an elect race embracing all nations in the New Testament. So here is a good start—*man was made to give glory to God.*

Whichever way you move out of Isaiah 43, sooner or later you will be confronted with this great principle, that man was made to give glory to God. Think of Daniel 5 and Belshazzar carousing with his lords and ladies. The prophet delivers God's judgement upon the king and he could have charged him with all kinds of sin but he went to the heart of the matter, to the fundamental thing: "The God in whose hand thy breath is, and whose are all thy ways, *hast thou not glorified*" (v. 23). Think of Acts 12 and King Herod. When he exalted himself the divine judgement came upon him swiftly. It says: "And immediately the angel of the Lord smote him, because he gave not God the glory" (v. 23). Leave the kings and come to the common people. They are gathered together in Romans 3. At the conclusion of a full length portrait of failing man Paul says: "For all have sinned, and come short of the glory of God" (v. 23).

Examples of success are measured in the same way. In Romans 4 it is revealed about Abraham that "he staggered not at the promise of God through unbelief; but was strong in faith, giving glory to God". Even Jesus Christ himself, the sinless one among the sinful, even he is valued by this measurement. In Philippians 2, Paul, describing the exaltation of Jesus, says "that every tongue should confess that Jesus Christ is Lord, to the glory of God the Father" (v. 11). Then finally, coming back to Revelation 14 and the day of enforced humiliation, the angel goes forth with man's last chance— the everlasting Gospel. He says with a great voice: "Fear God, and give glory to him; for the hour of his judgment is come" (v. 7). So all through the Bible in one form or another, this great principle keeps emerging: man was made to give glory to God. The question is, what does it mean in practice?

Creation Glorifies God

The Bible speaks about the created things giving glory to God. "The heavens declare the glory of God; and the firmament sheweth his handywork" (Psalm 19). "Praise the Lord from the earth, ye dragons, and all deeps: fire, and hail; snow, and vapour; stormy wind fulfilling his word: mountains, and all hills; fruitful trees, and all cedars; beasts, and all cattle; creeping things, and flying fowl . . . let them praise the name of the Lord . . . his glory is above the earth and heaven" (Psalm 148). So we sing about it sometimes:

103

> "Where'er we turn, thy glories shine
> And all things bright and fair are thine."

When Jesus, looking at the flowers, referred to Solomon's glory, he was comparing the glory of the king with the glory of God. How do the created things declare the glory of God? When they answer the law which God has put upon them and within them. When they are obedient to His design, that is, when they are what God has intended them to be—they give glory to their Creator. Upon every tulip there is the law of the tulip and when it blossoms in all its beauty it fulfils the law of the tulip—being what God intended it to be, it gives glory to Him. So with every eagle there is the law of the eagle and when it hovers in the heavens upon its great eagle wings, it is doing what God intended it to do and it is being what God intended it to be—true to its own law, it gives glory to its Creator. By these examples we come to man.

The Law of Man

Man is not a beast. In one respect he has no pre-eminence over a beast in that he is mortal, but he is not a beast. Your conscience will tell you. See a horse chained to a plough and you are exhilarated. The horse is doing what God intended it to do and you feel it is good. See a man chained to a plough and you are at once ashamed. Man was not made to be like this and you feel it is wrong. See a pig wallowing in the mire. You are not disturbed. You may not like the smell but your spirit is not offended. But see a man like this and you know at once that he is degraded. You know in your heart that it is wrong. Men are not beasts—and when they are beastly we say it is unnatural.

The Creator's thought for man is in His word. It says that man was made in the image of God. The powers that make man unique were given him to enable him to give glory to his Creator. These powers, the capacity to love, trust, assess and respond, which place man at the summit of creation, enable him to be true to his own law. Upon the tulip, the law of the tulip. Upon the eagle, the law of the eagle. Upon man, the law of mankind. When men answer the law of mankind they do that which is divinely natural and become like God. This was the issue in the beginning—man was faced with two possibilities, either to become like gods knowing good and evil or to obey God and eventually become Godlike.

Now manhood has been seen at its perfection but once—in the Man of Nazareth. He was the realised fulfilment of what God meant by "Let us make man in our image". When we look at the Man of the seamless robe we are looking at the archetypal man. When Pilate said, "Behold the Man", he did not know how truly he spake. This was a man submitted wholly to the will of God and dedicated to the service of men for their salvation; a man who laid the measurement of heaven upon earthly things. He handled and enjoyed the things of every day and looked through them to the spiritual. Birds: he said God feeds them. Flowers: he said God made them. Bread: he said there is a bread which gives life ever-more. Water: drink this water, he said, and you will never thirst again. The shepherd on the hillside: he said that God is a great shepherd and will not rest until the flock is enfolded. These things he did and we see in him the law of mankind fulfilled and realised. By this means he gave glory to God, and doing that he worshipped in the daily ministration of life.

In the Common Things of Life

What a solemn thing it is, this call to worship in the infinitesimals of every day. Either we use these unique powers to give glory to our Creator or the powers are prostituted. Prostitution is when the highest powers of man are used for the lowest purposes. Here is the solemn question—how was it yesterday? Was it a day of high purpose when even in the commonplace things of life the mind, heart and soul were in glad recognition of God's power and purpose? No hour in the day when to think of His presence caused a feeling of being ashamed? The powers of manhood used faithfully to give glory to God. Then it was a day of worship.

There is a psalm which tells these same things in a different way: Psalm 96. It is a psalm about giving glory to God, and then in verse 9 there are the words: "O worship the Lord in the beauty of holiness"—more proof, if it were needed, that giving glory and giving worship are equated.

Worship and holiness we have looked at carefully already in this book, so what we must give our attention to now is this unusual word beauty. We have seen that the beauty of the created world and the wonder of its myriad forms is an act of praise and worship to Him who made it all and sustains it all. A poet once described it thus: the soft beauty of the rose, the scented beauty of the honeysuckle, the strong beauty of the horse, the flashing beauty of the trout, the shimmering beauty of the stars and planets, all these praise the God who made them and conceived them.

The Psalmist is saying that there is another beauty which gives glory to God and gives Him worship—the beauty of holiness. The essential intention of the word used here is that the beauty is internal. Isaiah uses the word beauty when in chapter 61 of his prophecy he says that God will give to the mourners beauty for ashes. That beauty is external, something put on like a crown or a garland.

The Beauty of Holiness

But this beauty, the beauty of holiness, the expression of worship, is something which breaks through from inside. It is centred in a heart filled with reverent fear, seeking to discover the will of God and to answer it in humble joy; a life trembling at His word and responsive to His command; walking in the way of God's appointment, whatever it may be, like sheep content with the pasture which the shepherd has selected; a life of holiness unfolding the beauty which glorifies God.

The phrase occurs in Psalm 29:2, one more proof that worship is achieved by giving glory to God: "Give unto the Lord the glory due unto his name; worship the Lord in the beauty of holiness." If we seek to do the first in the regular exercise of the life of faith, we shall thereby worship the great God in the daily experience of discipleship.

Psalm 115 reveals a great principle—that men become like the God they worship, false or true. The end of true worship is Godlikeness. This principle is at the root of a great New Testament word: "We shall be like him." But one thing is essential—that the worship is true.

23

WELL-DOING

ALL true disciples would acknowledge that well-doing is an essential part of the discipline of Christ. The passage that comes to mind most readily is Galatians 6:9: "And let us not be weary in well-doing: for in due season we shall reap, if we faint not." The context is an agricultural one, emphasising that what men reap is what they have sown multiplied many times. Sow to the flesh and you will reap corruption; sow to the Spirit and you will reap life everlasting.

In the passage in Galatians the value of the reaping is a measurement upon the quality of the sowing. Because the harvest is so good the well-doing is no paltry thing. Eternal life does not issue from forces which are temporary, half-hearted, lukewarm and dilatory. The disciple's expectation towards age-abiding life is regulated to some extent according to his participation in the labour. In the day of harvest every labourer will need the mercy of God, but notwithstanding, sowers are expected to be persistent, faithful and industrious. Sowing is an act of faith. It is done hopefully, trusting that God will do His part, giving the increase and making harvest.

An Abundant Harvest

James says that the husbandman waiteth for the precious fruit of the earth and is patient over it. We must not put too narrow an interpretation upon the figure. Although the application is personal we must not look to the harvest as an opportunity to gain a great reward for ourselves. Individual saints will be rewarded with eternal life—a blessed gift from God, but the harvest is broader than the destiny of any one individual.

The hope of harvest is not selfish. It is a multiplied blessing for all. It is surcharged with God's love for man in need. It is the realisation of the Divine purpose, to make man and be manifested among them and in them—men and women co-operating with and revealing God; the grace of God outshining in the world. This is the harvest; this is the reaping. The point to be stressed is that since the harvest is fraught with love and compassion, so is the well-doing, or it should be.

The word translated "well-doing" in Galatians 6:9 is an interesting one. W. E. Vine says it denotes that which is intrinsically good, fair, beautiful. It means doing things which are honourable and noble, things which are ethically right. It has in it the idea of that which is well adapted to its circumstances or ends.

The Nature of Well-Doing

It comes out well in a passage in Titus 2:14: " . . . who gave himself for us, that he might redeem us from all iniquity, and purify unto himself a peculiar people, zealous of *good works*". Similarly in Hebrews 10:24: "And let us consider one another to provoke unto love and *good works*". We began the chapter saying that there would be unanimity about the need for well-doing, but we have to say now there would not be unanimity about the nature of the well-doing.

This is understandable. The word is expressed but it is not defined, and so disciples are entitled to use their judgement. It seems evident to the writer that the best good work that any disciple can do is to bring the Gospel to lost souls. This transcends all other well-doing. Paul said he was a debtor to the Greeks. It means he regarded himself as being in debt to any man who was without salvation. Well-doing is to do that which is honourable and there is nothing better than honourably to discharge that debt. To have that opportunity and to neglect it or spurn it is to be in debt dishonourably.

To revert to the Galatian figure, it is sowing seed into what may look to be dead earth on dark days with no sign of life, toiling and waiting in patience for the emerald sheen. The landscape is bare, the wind bites, the sky is heavy and the sluggard is at home. This is well doing in the best definition of the word. It is intrinsically good, fair and beautiful. "How beautiful are the feet of them that bring good tidings." It is well adapted to the circumstances. Where there is an urgent need there must be an urgent remedy. It may even be sacrificial. They that sow in tears shall reap in joy. Remember the leaden clods, the barren land, the cold drill, the inert seed—these are the very elements of harvest. Without them there would be no golden fruit.

Well-doing and Works of Mercy

It is recorded of the disciple's Master that he went about doing good and many who seek to live the life of faith are convinced they ought to follow his example. It means that in addition to preaching the Gospel they feel constrained to engage in works of mercy, helping those in need and showing compassion to those who are bereft.

This conception of well-doing is not without foundation. Once the King was interrogated by a lawyer about gaining eternal life (the very same harvest referred to in the Galatian letter) and the discussion developed into an account of a man who acted towards another with loving compassion because of his need. Jesus concluded by saying to the lawyer: "Go thou and do likewise." This record is in Luke 10, the story of the good Samaritan. It teaches us a great deal about well-doing, especially that if it is to be any good it may cost us time, money, trouble and inconvenience. Then next, this—that my neighbour is the man who shows mercy in my need. But also that my neighbour is the next man I meet who is in need and by whose need I am moved with compassion. Furthermore, he does not cease to be my neighbour just because he is a stranger or does not share my loyalties or convictions. Indeed he might be doubly my neighbour if his need is neglected by others.

The details of the story Jesus told do emphasise that real well-doing may mean going further than the conventional standard of helpfulness. A polite enquiry and a quick get-away is not really what Jesus meant by "do likewise". So, trying to be perfectly fair and without prejudice, it looks as though, according to the King's definition, my neighbour is someone in genuine need and especially if, being in need, he is also helpless. Because of the nature of the lawyer's enquiry about gaining eternal life, the matter cannot be regarded as peripheral. It is not something to be passed over casually nor something to be rationalised, as it sometimes is. It should be pursued not postponed. The next practical question is—in what way and by what methods?

A passage in the opening verses of Matthew 6 gives us clear instruction about how we ought to perform this kind of well-doing. It can be summed up by the words: "Let not thy left hand know what thy right hand doeth." It means when we arrange to do good works they must not be done ostentatiously but as far as possible they must be done quietly and secretly. Efficiently by all means; lovingly by all means, but as far as possible unobtrusively. That may mean works which are done on one's own or with another rather than in a crowd.

Motive is Everything

The writer's experience tends to convince him that working in pairs is best. There are some circumstances where well-doing has to be done alone but in general two souls joined on the same act of loving service usually brings blessing. In this matter *motive is everything*. Jesus said: "When thou doest thine alms, do not sound a trumpet before thee." This has reference to a fact, for this was the very thing the Pharisees did. Jesus said this displeases God. It is out of harmony with His purpose. He has to do with hidden things.

These are the things which please God—doing things secretly for men, giving, praying, self-denying. The need for secrecy ought not to stop us doing good works or being kind but to show us how to do these things in the right way. It would be a prostitution of the Lord's words to say that as we cannot do this good thing in absolute secrecy therefore we will not do it at all. The good Samaritan could not observe absolute secrecy in what he did, but what a travesty of the position it would have been if for that reason he had left the man in the ditch.

So whatever your reason may be for not doing some act of kindness, let it not be that somebody may find out. It is better to take the risk and act lovingly. Let us not be reluctant because the needy one is a stranger. Never in the New Testament is this offered as a reason for holding back a kindness. Indeed there is a suggestion that the needy stranger may be influenced by your compassion.

So the teaching about well-doing at this level is that, given the right safeguards and the true motive, it is definitely a part of true discipleship to engage in works of mercy towards those in need.

Not grudgingly but cheerfully; not in theory but actually; not for self-esteem but for love's sake. Furthermore, not by neglecting other important things in the Truth—but by sparing more of the time we use for our own things.

The Peril in Well-doing

Notice the danger outlined in the Galatian letter. It is not contamination, nor distraction, nor dilution of resources. It is weariness and fainting. Weariness is not tiredness. There is no defence against tiredness but weariness must be resisted. Tiredness makes us rest to be fit to work again. Weariness is losing heart and losing hope. It is sighing instead of singing. It is ceasing to believe in the emerald sheen. It is to relax through pessimism.

By weariness the sharp edge is blunted; shining faces are shadowed. So let every disciple keep bright the vision of the harvest and be forearmed against the assault of weariness and fainting. So we shall reap if we faint not.

24

UNITY

ONE of the most interesting expressions about unity is in
Ephesians 4:3: "Endeavouring to keep the unity of the Spirit
in the bond of peace." It occurs in a passage which has all to do
with practical discipleship. Such things as walking worthily; being
meek and longsuffering; forbearing one another in love and giving
diligence to keep the unity of the spirit in the bond of peace. In a
book about discipleship its omission would be reprehensible.
Evidently it is not something which is casual or incidental. Nor is it
the objective of the few who may have a special disposition toward
ease of mind. According to verses 7 and 13 it is the concern of all.
"Each one of us" is involved "till we all attain unto the unity of the
faith".

The Unity of the Spirit

The first thing is to be sure about what the apostle Paul meant by
keeping the unity of the Spirit in the bond of peace. It could be
argued that unity of the Spirit means simply spiritual unity.
Spiritual unity is very valuable, properly understood, but in this
case the words seem to unveil something very precise about the
nature of the unity. What is intended by the word Spirit in verse 3?
Notice there follow seven manifestations of unity—one body, one
Spirit, one hope, one Lord, one faith, one baptism, one God and
Father. It seems clear that the word Spirit here means the Holy
Spirit and not just a spiritual disposition. It seems reasonable to
conclude that the meaning of verse 4 is also the meaning of verse 3
and Paul is saying that disciples must give diligence to keep the
unity of the Holy Spirit in the bond of peace.

What did he mean by unity of the Holy Spirit? Almost certainly he meant the unity which is created out of submission to the Holy Spirit's revelation. As and when disciples accept without reservation the teaching of the Messiah, the prophets and the apostles, they are made one in faith and practice. Notice that disciples are not exhorted to create the unity, they are exhorted to keep it. It is already created by the act of submission to the Holy Spirit's teaching. Unity cannot be created by making arrangements or by building some organisation. Arrangements and organisation are important as means for disciples to make their submission and confess their agreement, but the unity is not created by the organisation; it is created by the one revelation of Truth, through the Holy Spirit.

Members Together

If proof were needed, the words at the end of Ephesians 2 are powerful. The people whom Paul is exhorting to keep the unity of the faith are those who have become fellow-citizens with the saints, and members together of the household of God, being built upon the foundation of the apostles and prophets, Christ Jesus himself being the chief cornerstone. In short, all those who are in Christ are joined together in spiritual unity.

Because these Ephesians had believed the Truth they were now part of the one body and in unity with all others who believed the same message of salvation. Because of this they were urged to preserve the unity, and they were to do it with all diligence. It was to be no milk and water assignment. They were to be guards protecting the one faith; sentinels over the union of believers. To the Romans Paul used some strong words to enforce the solemnity of this ministry: "Mark them which cause divisions . . . and avoid them. For they that are such serve not our Lord Jesus Christ, but their own belly; and by good words and fair speeches deceive the hearts of the simple" (16:18). These incisive words put a very high value upon spiritual unity and reinforce the exhortation in Ephesians 4 to give diligence to keep it.

There are, it seems to the writer, two kinds of unity. The first might be called the unity of absolute identity: the situation where every separate part is exactly like every other part; a comprehensiveness born out of precise uniformity. The pebbles on a beach

113

might be an example of this category of oneness, or the grains of sand in a child's seaside bucket: a monotony of sameness, a merging of dullness.

Some might want to argue that such uniformity is not real unity—that you cannot create oneness out of unchanging repetition. There may be something in this argument: perhaps there is a difference between unity and mere aggregation. But we must leave the purist to argue it and come to the second kind of unity.

We call it the unity of singularity—that is, the joining together in one of things which are dissimilar and different, a harmonising of forces which at first are disparate, a unity which is manifold. This is the unity of Christ's body, the unity of the Spirit. Think of the figure which the apostle Paul uses to teach us this truth—the limbs and members of the human body: different and yet having one cause, dissimilar and yet existing for one purpose, distinct and yet with one identical interest. The foot is not the eye; the hand is not the ear. Paul says there are many members but one body, and he insists that it hath pleased God to order it in this fashion.

So let us understand it rightly. The unity of the Spirit is not absolute uniformity, but it is the harmonisation of different forces brought together for a common purpose and in the realisation of that purpose made one. This is the unity of the Spirit.

The Affinity of the Father and the Son

John 17 and the great prayer prayed in the upper room can teach us about the unity which ought to exist among disciples. In verse 11 there is the record of Jesus praying for the disciples to his Father and saying, "that they may be one, as we are"; and again in verse 22, "that they may be one, even as we are one". If we can understand the unity that exists between the Father and the Son we shall know something about the unity which ought to exist between disciples.

Observing reverently the ministry of the Son and his God-mastered life, it is evident that the two were united at the highest level, that is, they had the same desire and willed the same things. The efforts of the Father and the Son were united in purpose and direction and in the final and ultimate objective. The Father's will was the Son's will; the Father's desire was the Son's desire; the Father's destination was the Son's destination. This is not the unity

114

of exact uniformity. The Father is the Father and the Son is the Son—the persons are one but distinct. The affinity does not impair the identity. But the unity is perfect—at one in purpose, direction and destination.

Notice the crucial words in this chapter which fix the fundamental basis of the unity between those for whom he prays: "Neither pray I for these alone, but for them also which shall believe on me through their word; that they all may be one . . . " (vv. 20,21). The unity is created because they believe on the Son through the testimony of his apostles. The apostolic teaching is essentially the word of the Holy Spirit, so the unity which results is the unity of the Spirit.

Notice the apostle Paul in the Ephesian passage urges the disciples to keep the unity of the Spirit *in the bond of peace*. This word "bond" means that which binds together—it is used in one place about the ligaments of the body. He appears to be saying that the peace which comes from true unity will bind you together and enable the distinctive parts to work for the common good. There is the peace of inertia, the peace of stagnation. There is the peace of apathy or the peace which comes from appetite satisfied.

But this is not the peace which comes from unity. This peace is the harmony of opposing forces or the control of things which hitherto have been without concord. Real peace arises out of conditions where the very opposite was once possible. So Paul says, "Let the peace of God *rule in your hearts*, to the which also ye are called in one body; and be ye thankful" (Col. 3:15). Peace rules—that is, it brings into subjection all the turbulent and divergent things and makes harmony. Paul is saying that where this peace dominates and controls, the unity is guarded and kept.

A Solemn Responsibility

No true disciple can be careless about the command to guard the unity of the faith. The body of Christ is not to be treated like a carcase—fit for butchery. The head of the body is the living Lord, the firstborn from the dead, rich with effulgent glory. It is no light thing to divide that which is unified in him. There is one head and there is never a hint in the New Testament that there is more than one body. All those in that one body have spiritual unity—national barriers cannot deny it and distance cannot harm it. It is built on a foundation laid by God and not by man, the things which are at the very centre of our faith.

Recollect thankfully what they are: the faithful ministry of the word, so that we shall not teach and lead by our own wit and wisdom but by the power and wisdom of the Word of God—the first and final source of authority; the faithful proclamation of the truth about the kingdom of God and the values of that kingdom which we are urged to manifest to those around us; the laws of spiritual life and conviction, teaching us how to live godly in an ungodly world; the sympathetic priesthood of Christ and the right of access to the great God of heaven, through prayer and communion by way of the one mediator; the powers and forces of our brethren and sisters, helping, healing and encouraging all those in need. Because of the exaltation of Christ we have need of no other head: no pope, no vicar, no synod. Resting firmly on the fundamental things and exercising faithfully the central things, there is that peace which binds together the faithful in the unity of the Spirit.

In Ephesians 4:4 the apostle Paul makes a categoric statement—short and unmistakable: "There is one body." Of that one body Christ is the head. If there are two bodies then one of them must be headless. The head cannot be divided. There were divisions in Corinth and it was the cause of grief to the apostle Paul. Is it not certain that what caused grief to the apostle would also cause grief to the apostle's Lord?

So at the risk of wearying the reader it is necessary to re-emphasise this one thing: the disciple must strive earnestly to keep the unity of the Spirit. The apostle said it categorically. It is no light thing to countenance division. A head that is not divided with a body that is, appears to be an awful contradiction. The New Testament makes no provision for such a possibility. What a splendid thing it would be if without the violation of any part of the truth and without the diminution of any aspect of the central things, the barriers could be broken down and the wounds healed, so that when the head comes his divided body was entire.

25

DAILY EXERCISE

WHETHER exercise is the right word the reader must judge. We toyed with action, practice and experience, but in the end settled for exercise. In any case the intention is to convey the idea of the fulfilment of discipleship in the routine affairs of daily life. Occasionally there are the volcanic and meteoric things, but these are exceptional. In the main, discipleship is practised in the ordinary things of daily existence. The value of discipleship may be superlative, but it is realised most in the realm of the commonplace. It has been stressed already in this work that if the disciples wait for the exceptional to prove their worth, they may well find that the opportunity comes too late for them to achieve the best. The essence of the life of faith is to do the next thing gladly and faithfully, not minding how ordinary it may seem. So this is what we mean by exercise: the habitual regular practice of the Master's principles in the ordinary affairs of everyday.

It is fairly common for people to measure their living in weeks. They say it has been a good week or a bad week. There is Biblical precedence for this. God spent a week creating the world and then rested. When disciples meet on the Lord's day they pray for help and blessing upon their ways until the next Lord's day. The regularity of ecclesial service is measured weekly in most cases. Sunday services, Bible Class, Youth Circle meetings occur in weekly sequences. All this is written to emphasise that it is often useful to measure the value of our discipleship by a weekly assessment of how things have gone. Of the 168 hours of the week, some are spent in the activity of our profession or our job; some in the

117

home; some in the service of the ecclesia and some in leisure. How many hours are spent in each avenue of activity will be regulated by the individual circumstances of each life. The point to mark is that each aspect of our weekly life is also a test of our discipleship.

Home, Sweet Home?

How we behave in the home, how we act at work, how we serve in the ecclesia and how we relax in leisure are all related to the master principles of the faith. No activity permits us to live incognito. However diverse the activities, we are the same individuals. The man who worships on Sunday may be in very different circumstances on Monday, but he is the same man essentially. He discovers that what is easy in the temple is not so easy in the marketplace. The reader must be patient with this statement of the obvious but it is presented in order to stress that sometimes people are tempted to change their manner of life when they change their location or their overcoat. It has happened that saints in the ecclesia are rather unsaintly in the home. The fact is that in the home people have no need to put on a performance. There is no call for window dressing. As they are, so they behave. It is an old saying that you have to live with people to know them. Where people live the restraint is eased. The outward show is relaxed. The solemn truth is that when we are not on show the truth about us is shown more surely. That is at the root of the old saying.

It may be hard to face but if discipleship fails at home it is not likely to be at its best anywhere else. Of all the tests, perhaps the home is the most severe. But it works both ways—it may be severe but it has wonderful possibilities for right development. The writer remembers the case of a young man who came into the Truth from an unbelieving family. One day his mother said to him: "I do not know much about your new religion, but I know this: you are much easier to live with now."

The home is a nursery for divine service in the ecclesia. "Let them learn first to show piety at home" is the instruction of the great apostle (1 Tim. 5:4). So the exercise of true discipleship in the home will seek for good manners, loving patience, admonition without provocation and strength without acrimony. Home is a place of safety and security, of joy and fellowship. Too soon the old home will disappear, and the folks who made it will be gone.

Keep it good now so that the remembrance of it will be sweet.

The Disciple at Work

Two of the foremost reasons for working at a job or a profession are religious: "That they may adorn the doctrine of God our Saviour in all things" (Titus 2:10) and "That he may have to give to him that needeth" (Eph. 4:28). So there is a sense in which working is part of the spiritual life. All disciples will know that their religious calling ought to have a strong influence upon the quality of their professional competence and service. First of all, the work they do is done as servants of Christ and not just to please the boss or advance their own position: "Not with eyeservice, as men-pleasers; but as the servants of Christ, doing the will of God from the heart" (Eph. 6:6). This should outlaw shoddy, shabby work. A disciple should be able to hold up his work in the light of God's scrutiny and feel he has done the best his abilities allow. It goes without saying almost, that the principles of discipleship would not permit Christ's servant to climb the ladder uncaring of the effect upon others. For Christ's man or woman ambition can never be ruthless. Nor can they gain if it means that thereby they lose spiritually.

In all things to do with working for a living the principle of upholding truth should be paramount. If the reader is wondering what this could mean let him think of industrial relations. Too often it appears that the accepted method in negotiation is to twist the truth or misrepresent it or even suppress part of it so that the advantage may be gained or the opponent defeated. Truth is indivisible. You cannot uphold it in one place and dispose of it in another. Sometimes a true man or woman by their good influence can stop the corruption; by their sanctified common sense can halt the drift; by their courage can arrest the evil. Exceptional forces working for good in ordinary circumstances—the disciple at work.

Ideally the cause of Christ has top priority in the life of the disciple, and the cause of Christ is realised in the work of the ecclesia. But in practice service in the ecclesia has to jostle for time with the other activities demanding the attention of the busy disciple in a bustling world. To be fair there are circumstances where the claims of home and work must rightly take precedence over the claims of the ecclesia.

In fact, part of the genius of discipleship is having wisdom to assess rightly where the true priorities may lie. Great care must be taken to ensure that the claims of home and work and leisure do not rob the ecclesia of support and service which it needs and which, being the ecclesia of Christ, it deserves. The spirit which at Caesarea urged Jesus to spare himself (Matt. 16:22) is in everyone of us urging us to do the same when the circumstances are unpropitious or the other calls more attractive.

The voice is saying, Let somebody else do the work, or bear the burden or take the responsibility. More often than not it is just a whisper, but it sometimes has an effect and the priorities get muddled. The thing to remember is that this occurs not in some matter of great principle where people have to stand up and be counted—then the Truth comes first. It occurs mostly in the everyday affairs of ecclesial life where great principles do not seem to be involved or where no danger to the Truth is discerned.

Conflicting Claims

All these paragraphs set out to do is to urge disciples to look carefully at their list of priorities and the value they give to each cause. Through forty-five years of experience the writer has come to a conclusion, rightly or wrongly, that there are three main forces which affect support and service in the ecclesia: (1) jobs and professions; (2) homes and family; (3) geographical isolation. The proposal about this can be put simply: that carefully we scrutinise our motives and our reasons when as disciples of Christ we decide upon the top priority in any particular circumstance at any particular time. As circumstances vary it may be a daily or a weekly exercise.

Leisure is part of the life of discipleship. To deny it is to do the cause no real service. Ceaseless toil, without rest or recuperation, at last brings the very thing which harms the cause most: weariness and worthlessness. Human nature needs development of a balanced kind. To over-develop one part of it so that another is wrongly contracted may in the end produce a damaged personality. To put it bluntly, man needs restoration to keep him well and whole. It is a divine bestowal that man should rest and have opportunity for leisure. The Sabbath was made for man. The doctor knows that sometimes exercise and play are better than his pink pills. Often to frolic is better than to fret. Laughing is better than loafing.

Discipleship is concerned with the highest development of those who are called, and towards that objective they must have relaxation. There are no rules about leisure, but there are principles which teach us the right from the wrong, the best from the worst. No relaxation which seeks to help one part of our nature whilst harming another part can be wise. No leisure which in pleasing us harms someone else can be right. No entertainment which, supposing to satisfy us, degrades those who perform it can be acceptable. Play should never be destructive; where possible it should always be recreative.

Recreation and Reverence

It cannot be expected that every form of enjoyment will make us better spiritually, but it should not make us worse. It cannot be said that every kind of play will deepen our reverence for God's Word, but what can be said is that it should never diminish it. The Bible does not tell us about cricket or croquet; about Bach or Britten; about pop, or painting or pottery as forms of recreation. But it does tell us about purity and fidelity and integrity, and with these things our discipleship is concerned every day. Finally, no leisure is right if it prevents us from being where God wants us to be or if it leads us where God wants us not to go. The writer remembers once hearing from a man in Christ about an occasion when he was in a certain place and someone said to him: "I am surprised to see you here; I thought you were a Christadelphian." The disciple told the writer it was like the cock crowing.

No day passes which is exempt from the master principles of the high calling. Discipleship is no small thing. It affects everything in its compass. There are no vacations, no retreats, no day-release. Our neglect does not lighten the responsibility; it may even intensify it.

Therefore, keep a keen eye upon the transaction. Make a weekly interrogation. Since last Sunday have the master principles of the calling fashioned, guided, regulated the exercise of living? Or in the busy bustling world were they submerged, perhaps even forgotten? Was there time for praying, for reading, for assembly with the saints? On the Lord's day, the day of rest, there should be time to make the assessment.

26

LEARNING AND WISDOM

IN this book it has been assumed from the beginning, of course, that the disciple is a learner and the Master is always the teacher. The manual is the Bible and the method of instruction is various and variable. It provides for group classes and individual study. The pupil is on his honour faithfully to pursue the discipline. There is no compulsion save the compulsion of love and loyalty. In this course of learning the principle of progress is simple. Success comes to the assiduous and the diligent. Spiritual poverty is the result of neglect and procrastination.

Whenever there is a cooling of enthusiasm, very often it is preceded by a famine of hearing the Word of God. Whenever there is a lack of gladness, very often it arises out of a condition of negligence in regular Bible reading. When the fires burn low it is because the disciple has defaulted in applying himself to the Word of Life. Every faithful disciple knows that learning from the Word of God is a vital part of progress and development. Remember the word of the great commission: "Go ye therefore, and teach all nations, baptising them . . . teaching them to observe all things whatsoever I have commanded you" (Matt. 28:19-20). Where there is teaching there must be those who are ready to learn. This may sound like a vague generality but in the genius of discipleship it is utterly central. Only by listening daily to the imperial voice of the Master will disciples truly learn.

The purpose of Bible study could well be defined as to increase and develop our knowledge and understanding of the Word of God. Knowledge is a vital thing. According to the apostle Peter the failure of the Jewish leaders was attributable to the fact that they were culpably ignorant (Acts 3:17). The charge of Jesus towards the lawyers was that they had taken away the key of knowledge. The apostle Paul confessed that he had confidence in the disciples at Rome because they were "full of goodness, filled with all knowledge" (Rom. 15:14), as though one could be traced to the other. Isaiah says of the Messiah that the spirit of God shall "make him of quick understanding in the fear of the Lord" (Isa. 11:3). What is true of the Master should be nurtured in the disciple. The advice of the wise man in Proverbs 4 is good advice: "Wisdom is the principal thing; therefore get wisdom: and with all thy getting get understanding."

The True End of Knowledge

The apostle Paul has some interesting things to say about knowledge in 1 Corinthians 8. The discourse in this part of the letter is about things offered to idols—something about which we may feel we can adopt an air of detachment. But the thing to notice is that they had knowledge in the ecclesia at Corinth. Paul says: "We all have knowledge." In some it was partial; in others it was advanced. Remember what this particular knowledge was about: the realisation of the futility of idols on the one hand, and the uniqueness and supremacy of God on the other. The apostle says in verse 7: "Howbeit there is not in every man that knowledge."

In this enquiry we must interest ourselves in those whose knowledge was advanced, not the weak ones whose knowledge was partial. Notice how the same knowledge among the advanced ones had different effects. With some it made them superior and being superior they were careless and indifferent as to whether their liberty might become a stumbling block to their weaker brethren. With others, and Paul was among them, it had the effect of provoking compassion for their weaker brethren and gave rise to a loving readiness to limit their liberty lest it should harm the brother who was weak.

The two different effects of having this knowledge are described by Paul like this: in one the ecclesia is puffed up and in the other the ecclesia is built up. As he puts it: "Knowledge puffeth up; love edifieth." The thing to mark is that it was not the nature of the learning which regulated the differing results; the knowledge was the same, puffed up or built up. It was the spirit, motive and purpose of those who learned it which conditioned whether it was to help or to harm.

This teaches us something we have always known: that knowledge brings responsibility and responsibility, unanswered, issues in harm—to ourselves and to our brethren. It shows that in the final definition true knowledge of God is more than an intellectual exercise. It is certainly that, but more, because it is possible for knowledge to be assimilated by a man intellectually yet not touch him volitionally. As one speaker put it rather clinically: the impact is cerebral but not cardiac. He went on to explain that there are some people whose minds are like lightning conductors as far as knowledge is concerned—that is, they are ready to catch the charge and carry it to earth as quickly as possible, and nothing inside is ever touched or affected. One writer has described it as sunshine passing through a block of ice and not melting it.

The truth is that knowledge of God needs to be assimilated by the whole man. It needs to reside in the spiritual centre, the place where mind, emotion and will all meet. The mind is illuminated, the emotions are stirred, the will is energised. With some at Corinth this had happened and with others it had not. It is when the knowledge of God touches a man's spirit that it communicates life and growth. It is in the recesses of the soul that the truth is either dynamic or doomed. True understanding is intended to result in pure motives and the purest motive is not to impress men with our intellectual superiority in Scriptural knowledge but to be well-pleasing to God. So disciples must take care to learn the meaning of this declaration: "Knowledge puffeth up, love edifieth."

Disciples with Heartburn

The report of the encounter on the Emmaus road is a revelation, as Luke tells it in chapter 24. Two disciples going home, sauntering home because there is nothing to hurry about. Their lives are suddenly sad, hopes are dimmed, their faith is expressed in the past tense. They said, "He *was* a prophet mighty in deed and word before God and the people". Jesus, travelling incognito, diagnosed their trouble. He told them they were suffering from slow hearts. Some people have trouble with palpitations, but these were in the opposite condition. In the life of faith, a slow heart is a heart that is never surprised, never amazed, never excited by the Word of the living God. These two disciples were thinking that it was all over and nothing was anymore worthwhile. So because their understanding was faulty their hearts were slow and their spirits were low.

Notice what Jesus did. He did not bring them any new revelation. He took familiar things and made them alive with a new meaning. Suddenly their hearts burned within them and the reason was that he opened to them the Scriptures. The things concerning Christ in the teaching of Moses and the prophets had the power to enkindle in slow hearts the heartburn which comes from God. And mark this, it did not happen while they were telling their doubt and asking their questions. It all happened when they ceased their sad complaint and listened to his exposition.

What a wonderful exegesis it must have been—an unveiling of the Messiah in the Hebrew prophets by the master teacher himself. Detect the excitement in their voice as they describe it: "Did not our heart burn within us, while he talked with us by the way, and *while he opened to us the scriptures*?" What a realisation! They had supped with the Emmanuel, the Branch of Righteousness, the plant of renown, the stone cut without hands, the child with the iron shoulder, strong to bear government, the man with beautiful feet upon the mountain publishing peace, the refiner's fire, the fuller's soap, the Sun of Righteousness. A new vision of old things: no wonder they had heartburn.

The new knowledge was not just intellectual, it was volitional. They sauntered out of Jerusalem but they went back at the double, filled with fire and fervour. Try to imagine how thrilled they were on the way back: mourning turned to joy in one evening; the brutal cross seen in a new light. By the Word of God the shutters were flung back.

The Treasure Hunt

In Matthew 13:52 the King explains something about the nature of discipleship. He says: "Therefore every scribe who hath been made a disciple to the kingdom of heaven is like unto a man that is a householder, which bringeth forth out of his treasure things new and old" (R.V.). Part of being a disciple then is seeking treasure in the place where God has hidden His riches. This sentence could well be interpreted in the light of the two disciples on the Emmaus road.

When Jesus said things new and old he did not mean some things which are old and some things which are new—two sets of things ancient and modern. Measured by Luke 24 he meant that the old things and the new things are the same things: old things seen with a new insight; new things revalued in the light of old visions; old things interpreted in the unveiling of a new experience. A new discovery out of the old treasure; ancient history opening new pathways; old rituals provoking a new reverence; old laws confirming new commandments.

This is the wonderful thing about the Bible. It is old and yet it is always fresh. We are familiar with every chapter and yet it is constantly surprising us. We travel through old country and each time find some new landmark. Time and time again we discover some radiant revelation of the wonderful purpose of God. No man, be he ever so good and ever so bright, has perfectly discovered the full treasure which has been submerged in the living Word. That means the treasure is never exhausted and always revealing something new and yet old.

The Renewing of the Mind

When the spirit gets pessimistic the best place for revival is in the optimism of the faithful Word of God. When the chariot wheels seem to flounder in the forward flight, there is release in the promise and provision of the perfect victor. No man can be sure of Christ until he is sure of Christ's word. He does not have to ascend into heaven nor descend into the deep to find it. It is there on the parchment of the book. Not written on tables of stone but written by the perpetual inspiration of the Holy Spirit in a form which ordinary men can handle and use, day in and day out, for their soul's sake. It is our consciousness which controls our conduct and our conduct fashions our character. The daily influence of the Word of God changes our consciousness and if the process is not impeded the right consequences will follow. In the word of Paul, there is a transformation by the renewing of the mind.

Jesus said it was possible for a man's mind to make him a sinner and just as truly it is possible for a man's mind to make him a saint, if the will is energised. The Hebrew man told it in chapter 9:14: "How much more shall the blood of Christ . . . cleanse your conscience from dead works to serve the living God?" The word conscience in this verse means the whole content of the mind—rightly our consciousness. Through the poverty of Christ many have been made rich, but the treasure does not fall from heaven in a golden casket, labelled and delivered to the front door. Like all good treasure it has to be sought with care and diligence. Remember Hebrews 11:6: "He is a rewarder of them that diligently seek him." Disciples seek God in different ways but one certain way is by a regular persistent attachment to His holy Word. Pondered, rightly divided, reverenced and obeyed: this is treasure indeed.

The Wisdom from Above

Knowledge is not wisdom. A man may have knowledge and be unwise. He may be thoroughly orthodox and have no heresy, yet lack wisdom. In a sense wisdom is *acting* wisely. Viewed from one direction wisdom is always prudent—the opposite of wisdom is folly. In the context of discipleship the definition is simple—it means letting the truth pass into action. A man who speculates about the truth but never really does it is a foolish man.

This is the measurement of Jesus. In the parable of the two builders, both men received and understood the sayings of Christ: the wise man was he who heard the sayings and did them; the foolish man did them not. In the day of testing one house stood firm, the other was a heap of rubble. The conclusion is straightforward. True wisdom is bringing the human spirit into conformity with the Spirit of Christ, who is the Wisdom of God. The Wisdom of God is realised in righteousness, sanctification and redemption, each perfectly revealed in the King and Saviour. The foundation is righteousness, the method is sanctification, the outcome is redemption. The Wisdom of God fastens upon the broken and the bruised and the spoiled and remakes them for His high purpose.

Wisdom is also manifested in the way a disciple behaves in the commonplaces and crises of life. If he has kept close to the Word of God and realised its teaching in the experience of discipleship, he will be able to know how to live and how to react to the problems and possibilities which confront him from day to day. Sometimes experience can teach us a great deal but it can teach us a great deal more if the mind is prepared by a sound knowledge of God's will. When the King was tempted in the wilderness and was confronted by the adversary, he fell back for his defence upon the naked Word of God. As the Master is, so should the disciple be. So the lesson should be clear. The whole man is affected by the teaching of the Master. He did not say only, "Thou shalt love the Lord with all thy mind . . . " and leave it there, but he went on, "with all thy heart, and all thy soul, and all thy strength". He is urging us that a man ought to respond to God with the whole complex instrument of personality. When it happens this is true wisdom.

Practical Application

That disciples ought to handle the Word of God regularly and persistently is beyond dispute. All believers would assent to this proposal. But it is one thing to approve the theory and another thing to make it true in practice. Many disciples are hard pressed with the duties of home and family and careers and work. The will is present but the opportunities are hard to find. Heavy eyelids and sleepy minds are not the best faculties for pursuing the treasure hunt. An occasional "mugging up" is not as good as a regular "searching out".

Imagine this: suppose the Bible kept its own diary in this place or that. How often would it have to record, "Have been kept in the bag all last week. Taken out on Sunday for an hour, and on Tuesday for a quick reference. Am now mislaid under the newspapers." The writer is not unsympathetic—he knows well about the difficulties and the problems. Life can be so complex but occasionally the actual issues are simple.

So it is here. As we are Christ's disciples we ought so to arrange our daily living that there is time for his learning and his wisdom.

27

THE SUPREME TEST

THIS final chapter proposes that the supreme test of discipleship is to be discovered in some words of the apostle Paul in Romans 8:9: "If any man hath not the Spirit of Christ he is none of his." The sentence is startling because it is so emphatic and categoric. The absolute nature of the declaration must cause us to stop and reflect upon the solemnity of these words. It means that if the Spirit of Christ is altogether absent, then the exercise is empty and useless—having an external form, but inwardly wasted and lost.

What is meant here by "the Spirit of Christ"? John Carter in his book *Paul's Letter to the Romans*, page 78, proposes that the Spirit of Christ is a Christ-like spirit to be equated with the new creature created after God in righteousness and true holiness. A condition of character identified with the expression of Romans 8:10: "And if Christ be in you . . . " Paul once said, "Christ liveth in me". It means that the life of Christ was being repeated in his apostle. Progressively he was being faithful with Christ's faith, hoping with Christ's hope, loving with Christ's love, seeing life through Christ's eyes, serving with Christ's compassion, standing fast with Christ's resolution. "Christ liveth in me." In this way the supreme test is being understood here.

The writer realises that other minds may well have other understandings and other insights. But for this understanding he is fortified by something in the Gospel of Luke 9:51-56. Jesus and the disciples are on their way to Jerusalem. At a Samaritan village they are rebuffed. James and John want to bring down fire from heaven to destroy the villagers. Jesus said: "Ye know not what manner of spirit ye are of. For the Son of Man is not come to destroy men's lives, but to save them.'' At that moment there was no harmony between the Spirit of Christ and the spirit of his apostles. This passage reveals the Spirit of Christ as an internal condition, developed and nurtured by the teaching of the Master; a disposition, spiritual and spirit-led, by the Word of God; the tone, the temper, the dynamic force of life.

We have suggested already that an ordinary word for this exceptional condition is *character*. After all, the character of a person is expressed through his spirit, his disposition. Character is the revelation of what a man is—so is his spirit. Here then is something to mark first of all from the emphatic statement of Paul. The essential and incisive test of what we are is discovered internally. Our spirit is the reality, good or bad. As a man thinketh in his heart, so is he. The external things we do occasionally are not the true measurement of our spirit, any more than the careful premeditated things we say. Occasionally hard men are kind, mean men are generous. God does not measure men by the occasional things but by the spirit.

In the Bible there are evidences that men sometimes act out of character. They do things which are out of harmony with their spirit. Abraham, the outstanding example of faith, falters and turns to a subterfuge when he thinks he may be in danger on account of Sarah. Moses, renowned for his meekness, in a difficult situation loses his temper. Elijah, the daring fearless prophet, flees in terror when he is faced with Jezebel's wrath. Peter, the man of rocklike courage, is vacillating and craven in the presence of the little servant girl. John Zebedee, the apostle of love, is calling down fire from heaven upon those who have rebuffed the King. It seems true—just occasionally people fail in a way which contradicts their character.

The Real Test

So not often do the occasional things reveal a man's true spirit. Just occasionally a person whose speech is usually pure and good will lapse into low language, or sometimes the opposite—a swearing man will utter holy words, but neither reveals the true spirit. The King once said that every evil word that men speak they shall account for in the day of judgement. Most disciples believe that a better translation is *every idle word*, because the idle unprepared word which comes from us artlessly reveals more truly the internal spirit. It is sometimes said, if you want to know the truth about somebody, ask the people they live with. This is more reliable than an official testimonial because it gets to the real man. All this stresses the need to look carefully at our internal spirit, if we are concerned with the supreme test of discipleship. In the words of the King, do we know what spirit we are of?

A useful measurement is to observe how we behave in unexpected circumstances, because usually at these times we have no opportunity to arrange our reaction or contrive our behaviour. Furthermore, very often along the line of the commonplace the truth about us inwardly is brought out. One writer has said that the Truth is like a winepress and the King is treading it. By his teaching and its effect in the disciples' lives he unveils their inwardness and reveals their true character. So the spirit is revealed in all kinds of developing conditions—sometimes in adversity, sometimes in prosperity, sometimes in obscurity and sometimes in popularity. In good times and in bad, among the ordinary things of a busy life, disciples discover of what spirit they are.

Developing Christ's Spirit

Since having the spirit of Christ is an internal condition, it follows that it cannot be achieved by a mere adjustment of external things. Tinkering with peripheral things will not change the things at the centre. Superficial forces will not accomplish radical changes. After all, it is the disposition that matters and that is not likely to be influenced by an admiration of the King's character only. The religious world is full of people who admire the Man of Nazareth. To admire and to discuss but not to submit is really in the end merely to patronise. Nor will it be accomplished by a kind of ritual imitation. A man may do externally the things which Christ did. He may go about washing people's feet, using only Bible words, speaking in the open and having no permanent home —and yet be not a true disciple for all that. Because, in the end, the real test is a test of the spirit. The heart is the place where the final judgement is made.

Think of the genius of discipleship, the transforming power which the first chapter sought to describe—its place of operation is at first the mind: "Be ye transformed by the renewing of your mind." At this level two important sentences come to mind: "Let this mind be in you, which was also in Christ Jesus" (Phil. 2:5); "Be ye renewed in the spirit of your mind" (Eph. 4:23). It may sound old-fashioned, but it is incontrovertible. As we let his words permeate our minds and as we let his deeds become the example and the experience of our daily living; as we recognise more and more the spiritual value of his teaching and as we realise the sacrificial quality of his love for our sakes, so we can gather for ourselves more and more of his spirit.

If anyone doubts that this is the method, think of the apostle Paul. He is wanting to urge the disciples to shed their meanness, to be generous, to give, even sacrificially, for their poor comrades in the faith. Notice his method: "See that ye abound in this grace also . . . for ye know the grace of our Lord Jesus Christ, that, though he was rich, yet for your sakes he became poor, that ye through his poverty might be rich" (2 Cor. 8:7-9). A changed consciousness results in changed conduct, which brings a changed character—changed in favour of Christ, his teaching and his spirit.

True disciples are constantly seeking to evaluate the essential elements of the Master's example. Jesus emerges from the Gospels as a man of clarity rather than complexity. He is open, artless, honest. There is no secret life which has to be concealed. The Spirit of Christ was one of transparent simplicity. He is never a man having to trim his words out of anxiety for his image. He is never looking sideways to estimate the impression he is making. He speaks openly, frankly and is prepared to imperil his life on the honesty of his teaching. It is like looking at the clear blue sky on a summer day, mistless and cloudless.

Next his composure. It shines out of the Gospel narrative every time you read it. Rarely is he compelled by circumstances, rather he is compelling the circumstances. When other men are excited and in turmoil, when other spirits are tempest-tossed, this man is serene. The last hour is the best example. Pilate is pacing the pavement and biting his nails; the people are restless and full of clamour; the priests are pugnacious and petulant. In it all there is one quiet, calm, serene spirit. It is the man of the seamless robe, the seer of Galilee.

132

Then his compassion. This is a signal revelation of his spirit. He responds with a divine naturalness to the sorrows and the joys of others. He is laughing at Cana and he weeps at Bethany. As he walked the streets and hills of Galilee the sensitivity of God was felt keenly among the people of Israel. In all their affliction he was afflicted. He knew that so often they were as sheep without a shepherd and he was moved with compassion.

This is one estimate of the Spirit of Christ—the Ideal. It is not the only one but it ought to be pondered because insofar as the forces of clarity, composure and compassion are developed in our character so Christ is in us. These things are utterly crucial in the exercise of daily discipleship.

What a problem the complexity of life can be! There is the spiritual and there is the secular and we have a foot in both camps. Too often the spiritual gets buried under the complexities of everyday existence. The issues, once sharp, get blurred. Things which once were clear are now complicated. Faith, once bright, is now dimmed. So here is the call—get rid of the things which encourage hypocrisy, and strive for the things which promote simplicity. Be done with the twilight zone. Walk in the light in clarity and be seen.

The Spirit of Restlessness

Think of composure. An outstanding feature of this age is its restlessness. It is part of the famine of hearing the Word of God. There is a phrase which has come to characterise the spirit of this age: "Must dash." It means there is no time for the timeless things and no time for the pleas and problems of the saints. Are you anxious over too many things? In the flow and flux of everyday life are you at peace? To put it plainly—to the extent that a disciple has the Spirit of Christ his heart will be fixed on the Lord: not mastered by panic but calmed by peace; undisturbed by being disturbed.

Think of compassion. It is love desiring the good of men in their pain and in their predicament. It is love springing up and running over for the sake of those who need salvation and life. It is sensitivity, moved, active and triumphant. "Let this mind be in you." Hardness is thus outlawed and meanness is banished. The compassion of Christ in his disciples will allow nothing radically to interfere with loving service towards the broken and the bereft. No personal preferences, no human pride, no superior wisdom, no love of comfort will hinder the sensitivity of love. Have done with your prudent calculations, with your confidence in the flesh; abandon yourself to the gracious example of the Redeemer. Have this spirit and you will be his, now and hereafter. This is the genius of discipleship.